A 365 DAY GUIDE FOR

Praising God

Happy 60th Anniversary
Alice & Ellsworth
with God's richest blessings
Theresa

May this book be a
blessing to you as
you read this together

A 365 DAY GUIDE FOR

Praising God

Paul Fellows

WORLD
Bible Publishers, Inc.

The author wishes to acknowledge use of material from the following:

The Holy Bible, published by the American Bible Society, New York, copyright 1873.

The Holy Bible, published by the World Publishing Company, Cleveland, Ohio, and New York. The book bears no copyright.

Goffine's Instructions on the Epistles and Gospels, the C. Wildermann Company, New York. Imprimatur New York, August 1893, and Permittitur Cincinnati, September 1893.

The Optimist's Good Morning, compiled by Florence Hobart Perin and published by Little, Brown and Company, copyright 1907.

Library of Congress Cataloging-in-Publication Data

Fellows, Paul.
    A 365-day guide for praising God / Paul Fellows.
        p.   cm.
    ISBN 0-529-06731-5
    1. Devotional calendars.   I. Title.
BV4811.F37   1989
242'.2—dc20   89-8453
                                                            CIP

This book is lovingly dedicated to my wife, Lillian. In this particular instance, her inspiration, guidance, and continuing encouragement have been more important than ever. There are truths, and truths, but it is more truthful than ever that this book would not have been possible without her.

The material is derived primarily from two very old Bibles. There were other very old inspirational writings used also. I then used my own feelings to modify what I read. I soon realized I was getting inspirational help from the Holy Spirit to such an extent that I sometimes wondered whether I was worthy and whether I could do the job apparently expected of me. The book, then, is the sum and product of my Christian life, and I am grateful for it.

Excerpt from March 11:

> *Let all who find you through me shout with delight.*
> *Let my voice be the most jubilant of all.*

Whoso offereth praise
glorifieth me.

Psalm 50:23

Preface

I was baptized a Christian on the second day of my life. I attended the school operated by our church and I received a wonderful basic grounding in religion, but religion was taught from the parables of the Bible rather than from the Bible itself. It was my great blessing to marry a girl whose religious training centered around use of the Bible. In the subtle ways of a woman and the gentle way of someone who loves me, she spent many patient years leading me to the Bible.

I began to read the Bible on a daily basis in 1985. When it sank into my consciousness that the Lord often said praise would please Him, I said to myself, "I guess that's fair." It did not take me long to learn that praises come awkwardly. Worst of all, once I developed a few, their repetitious use detracted from their effectiveness and even my sincerity. I developed a ten-day guide and used each day's phrases as my inspiration point. As an author growing in God and enjoying life more than ever before, the light finally snapped on, and this daily guide was born.

Finally, the commercial side of the book's birth had to be discussed. Following a phone call from my agent, I realized for the first time that the publisher had risks to consider. As I walked one morning, I said:

God, if there is a choice for me to make in facilitating its publication, I come down strongly on the side of reaching more readers and shifting financial risks over to me. You and I have lived through many experiences with this book. You inspired it, you let my eyes read my words and my fingers type the Holy Spirit's guidance, and you have shown me repeatedly how readily you've overcome obstacles along the way.

I prayed to you so often that the book would reach millions of persons throughout the world, so the miraculous process could begin. I asked that the greatest possible number, at successive levels, would use the book sincerely, accept you into their hearts, recognize your impact in their lives, see your goodness and greatness, recognize what little you ask of us, find you a very real and constant presence in their lives, and praise you joyfully.

I feel very blessed that God has chosen me as His instrument and allowed me to witness in this way. My faith tells me He will use this book to bring great honor to His name.

May the written text which follows for each day serve as your inspiration. Let it be the key to unlock your heart and tongue that you may praise him joyfully.

JANUARY 1

PSALM 111:2. The works of the Lord are great, sought out of all of them that have pleasure therein.

I look up, I look up. Your glory is my goal. I am thankful for my hope in you, Savior. I bless and acclaim you. I exalt you tumultuously.

You are so far beyond worth to receive my adulation. You are infinitely wondrous. My praise is but a feeble effort to measure your esteem.

My meditation of you is sweet, Ever Blessed Father. I am so delighted in your grandeur. All of my joys stream from your immortality.

Admirable Savior, I have peace with God through you. I pray to serve you well.

JANUARY 2

PSALM 148:7. Praise the Lord from the earth, ye dragons and ye deeps.

In your heaven, worship will be a perpetual feast of splendor. It gives me a new song, a delight to my soul. May the song resound in the hills.

The joy of a bride beautifies. How much greater joy there is in achieving passage through your gates; how much more beauty will abound there.

Heaven must be unspeakably glorious, for it is your home. The heavens beam with brilliant orbs. It is your reflection I can see, my celebration.

O God of Power, I pray for the good sense to be faithful to your promises.

JANUARY 3

PSALM 68:3. But let the righteous be glad; let them rejoice before God: yea, let them exceedingly rejoice.

I find perfect joy in my heart as I dwell upon you. May I be able and worthy enough to express my jubilation, my adoration, my love.

My small life strives to share your greatness. My heart strives to return the love you bless me with, measure for measure. I can only try, Lord.

Lord God of Splendor, I thank you for the goodness I do possess. I pray this will increase as I give others of my small store.

O Lord Jesus, take wide steps to my side. Help and comfort me always, and aid me in all endeavors.

JANUARY 4

PSALM 28:7. The Lord is my strength and my shield; my heart trusted in him and I am helped; therefore my heart greatly rejoiceth, and with my song will I praise him.

Let the saints be mirthful in their exaltation. Let their voices blend with mine in songs of rich celebration. Let peace reign everywhere.

Hearty praising is more wonderful knowing it pleases you, God of gods. I receive all my rejoicing from you, and return but little.

All the blessed privileges of the Gospel came through your priesthood. All of the foretold glories are seated in your kingdom. All honor is yours.

There is no purer way, no greater glory than in your light. Thank you for my salvation.

JANUARY 5

PSALM 25:1. Unto thee, O Lord, do I lift my soul.

In your light I see light. You are eternal, unchanging, infinite. You are power, goodness, truth, and justice. I offer you my adulation.

I can praise you with joyful lips, thinking of your distinction. I sing my songs of exultation, released by thoughts of your holy renown.

In the holy happy land of heaven there will be no sin and struggle. Your plan is divine and well worth the earthly struggle. You are merciful.

Precious Lamb, you laid down your life for me. I pray for the strength to please you with my life.

JANUARY 6

PSALM: 130:5. I wait for the Lord; my soul doth wait and in his word do I hope.

Full of trust, full of joy, my heart's delight is you. Your divine care and guidance open new doors. Your Precious Being is my exultant acclaim.

Following you, Master, has no equal. I love the angelic chorus praising you. My mind searches for more worshipful songs, Mighty Jehovah.

You complete my incompleteness. You change my restlessness to rest. I learned the sweet song of life loving you. I rejoice and I am glad.

God of Patience, you have counselled me wisely and steadily. I pray to live rightly in your glory.

JANUARY 7

PSALM 119:114. Thou art my hiding place and my shield; I hope in thy word.

Let me cultivate the best things within me. Let my voice, exalting you, wonder at the beauty and the excellence of your accomplishments.

May my richest motive be to please you. Great Counsellor, make each day blithe in duty. Sanctify my voice to venerate you better, Jesus.

I fear nothing and no one in my faith. My trust is in you, Preserver of Mankind. You make each day a time for rejoicing and gratification.

Good Shepherd, I am of your flock and following. Comfort me and deliver me into your presence.

JANUARY 8

PSALM 106:5. Let me see the good of thy chosen, that I may rejoice in the gladness of thy nation, that I may glory with thine inheritance.

I will find joy and gladness in extolling you. You bring forth splendid honor with your presence. You are the Fountain of Life, Jehovah.

Give me the Light of the Spirit, and the grace to trust. I will enter your gates with celebration. I will tell the sounding hills about you.

Eternal Presence of Holiness, my heart quickens at your blessedness. I can but return my delight in hymns of praise and honor to my Lord.

My Lord, my Shield, you adorned me with the innocence of life. My goal is to preserve my gift.

Praising God

JANUARY 9

PSALM 18:36. Thou hast enlarged my steps under me, that my feet did not slip.

I trust in you, Jesus, and I will never stumble or fall. I have your eternal word that I am of your covenant. I have your everlasting love.

You are my Rock, my fortress. I depend upon your steadfastness, God of gods; I look to your lovingkindness and marvel daily at your goodness.

The spirit of all hymns is for them to praise you, crown you, exalt you, and glorify you. May my voice lead the mighty chorus in jubilation.

Great Magnificence, you have been my strength ever. Continue to extend your mercy, Father.

JANUARY 10

PSALM 106:1. Praise thee the Lord; O give thanks unto the Lord for he is good, for his mercy endureth for ever.

Praise the Lord, you angels of His. Praise His eternal glory and greatness. Praise Him with me in a delightful refrain. Teach me your songs.

Praise you, Lord God of Hosts. Your majestic glory is absolute. Your wonders are emblazoned in the majestic skies you formed for us.

All glory to your name, You are always the same, Lord; before we were, now, and forever. What joy this assurance gives me. I know you live.

I will try to love you as you have first loved me. I thank you so much for your rich blessings.

JANUARY 11

PSALM 55:16. As for me, I will call upon God; and the Lord shall save me.

Come, O Christ, and loose the chains that bind me. My heavenly and real home is far removed in time, formed in wondrous magnificence.

Hail to you, Lord, who saves by your grace. Hail, all, join me to crown Him as Savior, Lord of all. Crown Him the Prince of Peace. Adore Him.

Sing to God, kingdoms of the earth. Sing praises to the Lord God Jehovah. Honor Him, all; extol His majesty. In wonder your wonders are mine.

God of Jubilation, I want my voice to lead the chorus of exaltation. I worship you, Lord of my life.

JANUARY 12

PSALM 145:13. Thy kingdom is an everlasting kingdom, and thy domain endureth throughout all generations.

I will spread my trophies at your feet. I will crown you Lord of the Universe. Your word is truth. I will crown you King of kings.

May every kindred soul ascribe majesty to you. Let me crown you Lord of all. Your goodness and greatness are forever, and they are mine.

You are the Good Shepherd. The Good Shepherd lays down his life for his sheep, as you did for me. Your lovingkindness is my life forever.

O God of Infinite Beauty, my days with you are a delight. Keep me safe in your light and grace.

JANUARY 13

PSALM 97:1. The Lord reigneth, let the earth rejoice; let the multitude of isles be glad thereof.

Holy, holy, holy Lord, all the saints praise and magnify you. My song is also for you alone, God. I praise you in the earth, the sky, the sea.

Let me crown you as the Virgin's Son, the God Incarnate born. You won those crimson trophies that we might not have to. Your love triumphs.

I will crown you Lord of Love. I behold your hand and side, rich wounds for your beloved. In beauty glorified, you are my mighty Lord.

Lord of my days, let the charm of gentleness enter into each service I perform. Let me witness widely.

JANUARY 14

PSALM 9:2. I will sing praise to thy name, O Thou Most High.

O God, create a new and clean heart in me. Fill me with clean thoughts and right desires. Let me live the knowledge of your eternal love.

Jehovah, my Light, my Strength, you are my high resolve. My praise is for you; my applause and esteem know no limits. May I always know your path.

I am happy in my search for ways in which to please and praise you. I am jubilant in my mirthful singing. I want always to joyfully love you.

*There is great joy in meeting a new day you have made.
I love you, Lord, with my whole being.*

JANUARY 15

PSALM 36:7. How excellent is thy lovingkindness, O God; therefore the children of God put their trust in thee.

Lord God, you are my Rock of Salvation. Help and bless me, and give me strength always. Let me please you in all I do, Father.

I can rejoice and be rapturous in my God. I glorify Him, for He has only lovingkindness for me. I laud you, exalt you, love you, Jehovah.

Great Spirit of Light and Love, in you is wisdom and strength. I find my path in your holy light, and salvation is the reward at the goal.

The sweet reward of your approval is my treasure. My pleasure and happiness come in serving you.

JANUARY 16

PSALM 84:10. For a day in thy courts is better than a thousand; I had rather be a doorkeeper in the house of my God than to dwell in the tents of wickedness.

You live to grant me rich supply. You live to guide me with your eye. You live to comfort me when I am faint. You live to hear my praise.

You are robed in majestic honor with light and glory. You stretched out the starry curtains of the heavens to let me see more of your wonders.

You hollowed out the surface of the earth to form the seas. The clouds are your chariots, in which you ride on the wings of the wind. You are God.

O Blessed Comforter, I think of you reverently and often. Bless and keep me, Lord God.

JANUARY 17

PSALM 16:9. Therefore my heart is glad, and my glory rejoiceth; my flesh also shall rest in hope.

All will be blessed in you. All nations will praise your name and acknowledge your wonders. You are Jehovah, the Light and Life of the world.

Let all the earth adore you, Lord, and sing tributes to you. Let me sing my psalm to your name. Let me magnify your excellence.

Shout with joy to the Lord, all you who live. Let the earth sing a song to your honor and glory. Give glory to His praise; there is no other.

The silent wonder of a morning is a new opportunity to serve you. May I meet that challenge well.

JANUARY 18

PSALM 22:28. For the kingdom is the Lord's, and he is the governor among the nations.

You are my food and drink, and my highest jubilation. You are my light in darkness. You give me broad steps to tread and to place my feet.

The angels and I praise you, Holy Trinity. You are good, and praiseworthy. Your mercy endures forever and I am yours, All-Loving Father.

Glory be to God on high. I adore you, my Lord, from whom all blessings flow. Your magnification is my goal in my daily attention and love.

Spirit of Holiness, your world is my gift. I want to enjoy its wonders while walking faithfully to you.

JANUARY 19

PSALM 5:7. But as for me, I will come into thy house in the multitude of thy mercy; and in thy fear will I worship toward thy holy temple.

Lord, you look down from heaven to see if any are wise enough to want to please you. I pray that my life is one of acceptance in your sight.

You are the refuge of the poor and the humble. Save me, Lord. I come for strength. I do want to strive for humility, and I pray for your help.

Adore God, angels of His. Earth, rejoice. Men everywhere, lift your voices in exaltation to the God of Righteousness and Charity. Worship Him.

My Protector, I have so much pleasure in you. You love me and show me continuous mercy.

JANUARY 20

PSALM 18:46. The Lord liveth, and blessed be my rock; and let the God of my salvation be exalted.

Everything was made for your glory, to display your greatness. All things bow before you; all worship is for you. Accept my resounding praise.

All things laud you, and I join in. I render glory to you, with the legions of angels. You are the Giver of life, the Redeemer. You are Jehovah.

My Light, my God Eternal, accept my thanks and praise. I glorify you for your goodness and greatness, for the rich wonder that is my Lord

Giver of all good, your greatness is apparent in so many things. I rejoice thinking of your holiness.

JANUARY 21

PSALM 33:1. Rejoice in the Lord, O ye righteous, for praise is coming for the upright.

My heart will rejoice in you. My hope is in your strength and goodness. May all persons laud and venerate your splendor and magnificence.

All my soul is jubilant in you, Lord. I am supremely joyous at your salvation. Let everyone be glad, and let everyone praise you mightily.

Dear Lord, help me to live more for you. Reveal yourself to me more each passing day, Redeemer. Let me remain your trustful child always.

God of Righteousness, you respond to everyone who asks. You are my eternal life and love.

JANUARY 22

PSALM 25:10. All the paths of the Lord are mercy and truth unto such as keep his covenant and his testimonies.

I know that all good men flourish. Everyone who knows you enjoys your abundant love and blessings. You are lovingkindness forever, Blessed Lord.

Praise my Lord, skies above; praise Him, vapors above the clouds. He is your Maker, your Lord Most High. Beloved Savior, you are Light and Life to all.

May everything and everyone you have made extol your glory. You commanded it and the world began; it is all yours. Hallelujah to the King.

Teach me to be more like you, Revered Lord. I want to follow you to your majestic throne.

JANUARY 23

PSALM 109:30. I will greatly praise the Lord with my mouth; yea, I will praise him among the multitude.

Fairest Lord Jesus, Ruler of Nations, you are God and man. You are Father, Son, and Holy Spirit in one. You are the paradise we strive toward.

I sing to your name. You are easy to honor and praise. You are so majestic that tribute and homage come easily to my lips. You are my God.

Praise Him, all, laud His glory. Extol my Lord's goodness and omnipotence. My heart is mirthful when I join the world in loving you.

Lord Evermore, let me always deserve your love. Make me steadfast in my faith.

JANUARY 24

PSALM 105:4. Seek the Lord and his strength; seek his face evermore.

O God of gods, my heart finds gladness in you. My voice can only exalt you to a portion of your worth, for you are far too magnificent to fathom.

Mortals can join the mighty chorus begun by your morning stars, while flowers unfold before you. Why wouldn't all the world wonder.

Be turned toward me ever, Father. I will be happy in you. Glory to you, God of the universe. I see only gayety and richness in my thoughts of you.

I pray to walk always, in peace and love, in the quiet ways illuminated by your glorious light.

JANUARY 25

PSALM 18:31. For who is God save the Lord, or who is a rock save the Lord.

O Lord God, never stay away for long. I need you always. I trust in you for all things. I pray I may have the good sense to accept your love.

I always expect you to help, Jehovah, and you never fail. You offered this in your covenant, which you keep so lovingly. You are my life.

You are good, and you do only good. I want to be led along your blessed pathways. I want to shout your gloriousness exultantly.

Blessed Presence, your hand of plenty is open in graciousness. You are holy in all your acts.

JANUARY 26

PSALM 27:8. When thou saidst seek ye my face, my heart said unto thee thy face, Lord, will I seek.

I want to serve in all ways through you, getting in order to give. I have a deep and exultant joy in you, Lord. You are my beckoning goal.

Peace and joy in you are mightily abundant, God of Hosts. No pleasure compares with pleasing, praising, honoring, and revering you.

I will crown you with many crowns as thrones fall before you. I will crown you King, the King of all. Accept my homage; accept my love.

Glorious God, you have provided me always with my needs. Let me learn to walk rightly in your vision.

JANUARY 27

PSALM 87:7. As well the singers as the players on instruments shall be there; all my springs are in thee.

You hear and respond to the cries of all in need, Great Jehovah. You bring solace and comfort, love and compassion. You are lovingkindness.

My tongue is full of your praises, my Lord. Fearing you, God, I have found a steadfast friend. You are the good things of life, earthly and eternal.

I sing songs of veneration to you, Jesus. I trust and rely upon you. All the earth is a Holy Land because of you, full of the redeemed you saved.

You are close to everyone, Lord, at the call of all. I want to please rather than to be pleased.

JANUARY 28

PSALM 148:3. Praise ye him, sun and moon; praise him, all ye stars of light.

I will tell everyone that Jehovah reigns supreme. He reigns in my heart and throughout the universe. He is my hope of life eternal.

I praise you for the growing fields. They display your greatness. May the trees of the forests of the universe rustle with your praise.

You are the Way, the Truth, the Light. Let happiness eternally flow. Grant that I may know. Let me keep that Truth and win that Light.

Esteemed Savior, I am trying to be worthy of you. I can try harder, and I pray for help to do so.

JANUARY 29

PSALM 69:32. The humble shall see this and be glad, and your heart shall live that seek God.

Be delighted in God in His infinite glory. The voice of your magnification, Lord, will be made to be heard. I will unburden myself of a joyous song.

Your wonders are majestic and enthralling. You are the Maker of the mighty deep, the heavens, and all the earth. You are the Great Creator.

You have shown me the way to your blessed eternity. You keep me in the righteous pathway. You are my central place of calm, my tranquil love.

Lord, you have done much for me, a sinner. Your love is the balm to heal a wounded heart.

JANUARY 30

PSALM 150:1. Praise ye the Lord; praise God in his sanctuary; praise him in the firmament of his power.

Let me sing merrily to you, God my Strength. Let me make a cheerful and exuberant noise before you. Let me pay homage to your greatness.

Praised be you, Lord Evermore. Let the delighted voices resound with ethereal joy. Let the earth extol and glorify your blessedness.

Your heaven begins in my soul, as an eternity of peace that can enfold it forever. I delight in you; I enjoy your presence. My praise is to you.

God of Consolation, you have blessed me in so many wondrous ways. My goal in life is to return some measure.

JANUARY 31

PSALM 29:11. The Lord will give strength unto his people; the Lord will bless his people with peace.

Blessed be you, God. Hosanna in the highest resounds from the holy mountain. Let heaven and earth rejoice in your richness; let everyone sing.

I will take pleasure in your Word. I will draw comfort from your counsel. You are the Perfect Being, the Lord of Life, the Supreme Ruler.

Awake, my glory, join in His praise. Sing to Him among the nations. Let the hills reverberate with my tribute to His wonder and splendor.

You are life itself, love, and honor. Continue, my Lord, to give me of your mighty graces and blessings.

FEBRUARY 1

PSALM 84:2. My soul longeth, yea, even fainteth for the courts of the Lord; my heart and flesh crieth out for the living God.

This is your world, my Father, let me never forget. All nature sings joyously to declare the glory of the Maker who made all persons and things.

You are the Ruler, God, the King of kings. This is your universe to command, and you are our praise. All of it is of your everlasting doing.

Sing, O my tongue, adore and praise my God. He brought the world out of nothing with His mighty power, and then saved it again for us. Praise Him.

I will take pleasure in your Word, and I draw comfort from your Being. You are my Radiant Lord, my prayer focus.

FEBRUARY 2

PSALM 25:8. Good and upright is the Lord; therefore will he teach sinners in the way.

How gladly nations sing for celebration. You are the King and Spirit. I rejoice to be able to extol your goodness and greatness.

Lord, you are the King forever and ever. Hallelujah, my Lord lives. You are still in your temple, and you rule from heaven.

God, you are so lovingly good, and you love goodness so much. The godly will see your face. You hold all of us safe from harm and bless us.

How great you are, God Almighty. Your deeds are abundantly good, and my heart and soul revere you.

FEBRUARY 3

PSALM 30:1. I will extol thee, O Lord, for thou hast lifted me up, and hast not made my foes to rejoice over me.

I am radiant with exultation because your mercy is unfailing. I am supremely happy in my love for you. I am delighted singing my songs of praise.

How great your goodness is to those who proclaim you. It is a pleasure and privilege to exalt and worship you, my Lord God.

Lord, you bless all who truly worship the Father. The majesty and glory of your name and presence permeates and enriches all the earth and heaven.

You justly judge all people and nations. I want to live so as to merit favorable judgment, Jehovah.

FEBRUARY 4

PSALM 119:7. I will praise thee with uprightness of heart, when I shall have learned thy righteous judgments.

There is joy in me to thank you publicly throughout the land. May your glory shine in upon everyone's heart. Let your rejoicing be strong in me.

O God, strength of my loins, I sing in exultation of your greatness. You are my secret place, my goodness, my light. Adoration is mine.

O Most Glorious God, the heaven of heavens cannot contain you. May my life show forth my adulation. My worship is intended to be precious to you.

Great Arbiter, you have bestowed favor upon me. Let my strength and love serve you better each day.

FEBRUARY 5

PSALM 34:3. O magnify the Lord with me, and let us exalt his name together.

The beautiful assurance of your love and kindness surrounds my magnifying acclaim. My merriment comes from knowing your love. You are my love.

It is a good thing to sing jubilantly to you, God of Patience. It is pleasant and gay to thank you for your plenteous goodness and grandeur.

I will sing to you, Jehovah, with thanksgiving. I will sing of your praiseworthy love and wondrous nature. I will venerate you in field and forest.

Lord God of angels, show me the threshold I must attain, and let my prayers invite the Holy Spirit.

FEBRUARY 6

PSALM 135:3. Praise the Lord for the Lord is good; sing praises unto his name for it is pleasant.

I praise you, Lord. You do miracles for me daily, and for all the world. You are the promised King, the Savior who serves in your covenant with us.

I worship you, Jehovah, God of heaven. The earth, the sun, the moon, the stars; all are yours. Your power cannot be understood by man.

Come with great power, God. Defend me with your glory and magnificence. Let your light for the world illuminate my way to you. Let me live in you.

We receive your generous blessings if we but ask. You are wonderfully good to all, Lord.

FEBRUARY 7

PSALM 59:17. Unto thee, O my strength, will I sing; for God is my defence and the God of my mercy.

God from ages past, hear my prayer. You are the living, ceaseless God, graciously magnified in my sight. Hosanna in the highest.

Saints of heaven, sing His praises. Remember His holiness with thanks and worship. He is joy, acclaim, happiness, and my heart's celebration.

I am glad and I rejoice in your mercy. My hope is in my living and loving Christ, Esteemed Savior of my life. Hear my tribute to your honor.

I will pray morning, noon, and night to you. God, my heart is an opening flower seeking you.

FEBRUARY 8

PSALM 138:4. All the kings of the earth shall praise thee, O Lord, when they hear the words of thy mouth.

I will go to the altar of God in my exceeding joy. I will praise what I know of God, understanding that I know really nothing of His greatness.

Love and joy seem immortal when they verge toward you. Eternal God, you are all of life. Let me love and obey your will, and extol your blessed name.

I praise you, Living God. The rain, the sunshine, the wise and wondrous ways you use the elements, are another precious gift. Your goodness is my joy.

My Maker, you are truth, light, honor, and forgiveness. I am walking your lighted pathways.

FEBRUARY 9

PSALM 80:1. Give ear, O Shepherd of Israel, thou that leadeth Joseph like a flock; thou that dwellest between the cherubim, shine forth.

Be joyful in the Lord, all. I pray everyone will serve Him with gladness and great joy. Come into His presence with songs of adoration.

I will follow the lighted path through the holy gates with thanksgiving, and go to your courts with praise. Your mercy is wondrous, Divine One.

You are the light of the world. As a follower I cannot walk in darkness but in exalting vigor, praising you. You are Magnificence.

I am blessed just to know you, Gracious Redeemer. I pray for your unremitting love to be love I earn.

FEBRUARY 10

PSALM 66:8. O bless our God, ye people, and make the voice of his praise to be heard.

When the birds wing their merry way, songs of rejoicing accompany them. There is nothing that can shut out the exultant bliss which flows from you, Lord.

My heart yearns to be pure for you; a contented spirit. My trust is in you, O Mighty Potter. In you I see that loving is more than enough.

You are my strength, Redeemer Lord. What glory you bring to all the world. My power waits on your favor alone. What rich joy you bring me.

Great and Awesome God, let love for everyone be my constant companion. Let me search and find your holy hill.

FEBRUARY 11

PSALM 46:10. Be still and know that I am God; I will be exalted among the heathen; I will be exalted in the earth.

You have heard my vow to praise you daily and often. You have given me the blessing reserved for your people. You are the Radiant Lord.

I will bow before you forever, Lord God. Send your truth and lovingkindness to envelop and shield me. Give me the heart to extend your love to all.

Your power and greatness, God, reach to the heavens. My song of tribute is trying to tell you of my jubilation at knowing you, Christ Jesus.

You shepherd me on the path of righteousness, God of all. Let me return my thanks in praise.

FEBRUARY 12

PSALM 107:8. O that men would praise the Lord for his goodness, and for his wonderful works to the children of men.

Because of your great power, Lord, I live. Acclaim and applause for you are my life's intent. Your splendor is exultantly praiseworthy.

May everyone everywhere bless you, Lord God, and sing your praises. I pray to join everyone in psalms and hymns extolling your greatness.

Magnify my Lord, everyone. He is the Lord Most High; King of the Universe. He is the centerpiece of the Book of Grace and the Book of Glory.

Your spirit is with me strongly, Jesus. Your holiness never changes. Let me strive more to honor you.

FEBRUARY 13

PSALM 150:2. Praise him for his mighty acts; praise him according to his excellent greatness.

The wonders of the earth speak to me in witness of your love. Springtime grass and opening flowers speak of my renewed hope because of you.

Joy is in the song of birds, the murmur of water, and children's laughter. Jubilation is in my heart at thoughts of you, Blessed Master of Life.

All the world worships you, sings of you, and lauds your greatness. The voice of acclaim is clear and strong, echoing from your holy mountain.

Omnipresent God, my happiness is in you and in obeying and worshipping you. You are my Lord, my life.

FEBRUARY 14

PSALM 30:4. Sing unto the Lord, O ye saints of his, and give thanks at the remembrance of his holiness.

Thank you, my Lord. I will sing exultant songs of adulation, daily and often. God above all, I strive to honor you. I can and will do more.

You forgive my sins unendingly, in your great mercy. You have shown me the way to be better, with the rich reward of eternal life. I will try.

You are the only hope of mankind. You provide a haven for me at your side in your holy home. All I need supply is love and the will to obey.

Let me love your commands and desire your promises. Your promises will be fulfilled.

FEBRUARY 15

PSALM 19:14. Let the words of my mouth, and the meditations of my heart, be acceptable in thy sight, O Lord, my strength, my redeemer.

There isn't time to tell of all your wondrous deeds. My life is worthwhile only because I praise your glory and know your wonders. You are love.

I delight to do your will, my God. Your law is written upon my heart with love. I rejoice in lauding your magnificence. My life is yours.

You have never forsaken anyone who loves you, Father. The children of such persons have not gone hungry. You are a considerate and loving Father.

Your blessed ones will inherit the earth, Dear Master. I pray to be in that inheriting number.

FEBRUARY 16

PSALM 45:6. Thy throne, O God, is for ever and ever; the sceptre of thy kingdom is a right sceptre.

Your glorious acts will startle people because of their majesty. Your miraculous deeds are awesome indeed. In love we can begin to understand.

O Lord, you are so worthy to receive the glory, honor, and adulation I have prepared for you. You are the Creator, God of gods, King of kings.

All things were made and called into being by your act of will. You reign over all, supremely. Your ruling hand combines power and love equally.

You continue to do all things for me. It is my turn to say, and mean, your will be done.

FEBRUARY 17

PSALM 39:4. Lord, make me to know mine end and the measure of my days; what it is, that I may know how frail I am.

I rejoice, Lord, I rejoice. You will see to it that fairness and justice always prevail. You have already decreed that we can find you.

Be glad, righteous souls, rejoice in my Lord and Savior. Be joyous. Sing, sing, jubilantly proclaim His glory. Sing your praises with good courage.

I am blessed, for my God is Jehovah. I can extol you and do honor to you by my daily living. I can adore your beauty and magnify you.

I pray everyone may constantly exclaim how good and great you are, joining in my rich celebration of you.

FEBRUARY 18

PSALM 140:13. Surely the righteous shall give thanks unto thy name; the upright shall dwell in thy presence.

Your thunder is in the heavens, Almighty God, the God of gods speaking. When you speak, your glory streams forth. I am blessed in your sight.

All the world sings with gayety, praising you. I thank you for all of my rich blessings. My esteem is of the highest order.

I sing rapturously of your holy name, telling the world of your wonders in my poor vision. I witness to your power and majesty.

Shepherd of All, you bring goodness, light, and love everywhere you touch. My fulfillment is in you.

FEBRUARY 19

PSALM 123:1. Unto thee lift up I mine eyes, O thou that dwellest in the heavens.

You have filled the earth with spectacular miracles. They still continue. Your magnificence never diminishes. Your glory only grows.

To you whom I adore, all praise and honor. I am saved by your holy grace. I live to love you, to know you better, to laud you ecstatically.

Spirit of the Living God, the joyful sound in the land is your glory. Christ, life of all the living, I wish to serve you faithfully forever.

I give thanks for my being, for my reasoning power, and all the magnificent endowments you gifted me with.

FEBRUARY 20

PSALM 145:14. The Lord upholdeth all that fall, and raiseth up all those that be bowed down.

Lord, you fashioned the hearts and minds of all; now guide me to wisdom in you. Let knowing more be loving more; let loving be praising more.

Sing to my Lord, O earth. Declare each day that He is the one who saves. His gentleness makes all people great; His salvation gives us life.

You are the Author and the Giver of Truth. My endless tomorrows will be joyous when my thoughts and deeds are truly dedicated to your worth.

My prayers are but a small tribute to your greatness, but they are sincere, my Lord.

FEBRUARY 21

PSALM 37:3. Trust in the Lord and do good; so shalt thou dwell in the land, and verily thou shalt be fed.

Invisible Presence, there can be no place where you are not. You are the beauty of the flower; you are what goodness there is in the human soul.

I sing to your praise, my Lord and Comforter. I am jubilant, knowing you. Rich delight is my portion because you are the Lord of my life.

My praises come out exultantly to Jehovah, who lives in the holy hill. I will tell the world about your unforgettable deeds, about your wonder.

Adored Father, may I always serve you with faithfulness and gladness; may my life itself be your praise.

FEBRUARY 22

PSALM 64:9. And all men shall fear, and shall declare the work of God; for they shall wisely consider of his doing.

May all the trees bow before you, Mighty Jehovah. May the rustle of the wind sing your eulogy in radiant song. Let your countenance bless me.

Believers need only to love you, Lord. Judgment will not touch them harmfully. You forgive and forget; only you can master that, in love.

There will be constant praise for you where I am. I will urge everyone to honor you in every way possible; in thought, word, and deed.

Infinitely Loving God, help me to live the life I should, and let me enrich the lives of others.

FEBRUARY 23

PSALM 40:16. Let all those that seek thee rejoice and be glad in thee; let such as love thy salvation say continually, Let the Lord be magnified.

I shout Hallelujah to your presence. Thank you for turning my life around so that I now see you. You are the inspiration of any good I do.

I will talk to others of your glory. I will laud your name before them. I will tell everyone of your majesty. I am so blessed to know you.

Every man must die after an earthly span. Breathing stops, life ends. In a moment plans are meaningless, but in Christianity a new life begins.

Everything you do is worthy of my homage. You are my life's delight, my Splendid Lord.

FEBRUARY 24

PSALM 134:1. Behold, bless ye the Lord, all ye servants of the Lord which by night stand in the house of the Lord.

Blessed be your glorious name forever. Let the earth be filled with praise to you, Jehovah. Lord of Hosts, you are divinity. You are life itself.

How good you are, Creator. All who strive to serve and please you are singularly blessed. To earnestly live in the Word is to extol you.

You are exceedingly wondrous, Ever Blessed Redeemer. You are clothed in splendor and righteousness. Your gentleness is my greatness.

Lord of Divine Greatness, you have made an everlasting covenant with me. I bring so little to the exchange.

FEBRUARY 25

PSALM 24:10. Who is this King of glory; the Lord of Hosts; he is the King of glory.

I rejoice to know your greatness. Your love for me is the eternal sun without eclipse. Life is in you; goodness and mercy come only from you.

Praise to you, God, Strength of my ancestors. You were here yesterday, you are here today, and you will be here tomorrow. You are unchanging.

I laud you, Christ Jesus, for demonstrating such loving-kindness to me. You are always wonderfully merciful, loving, good, and generous.

You heal the broken and the brokenhearted. You are the Lord; I kneel before you in adoration.

FEBRUARY 26

*Psalm 96:8. Give unto the Lord the glory due his name;
bring an offering and come into his courts.*

Lord God, you made heaven and earth to serve man.
You constantly keep your covenant promises even
when we err, return, and repeat the process.

Jehovah, you are the King robed in majesty and splendor. The world is your footstep and heaven your
throne. I pray to merit your eternity.

I have known your presence in so many ways. You are
the guiding hand, the joyful welling up of praise. You
are the Splendor of my days.

*You are always wonderfully merciful, loving, and gen-
erous. You are the Lamb of God, who is life to me.*

FEBRUARY 27

*PSALM 148:14. He also exalteth the horn of his people,
the praise of all his saints; even of his children of Israel,
a people near unto him; praise ye the Lord.*

You alone are God. You made the skies, the heavens,
the earth, the sea, the forests. You preserve it all.
May the angels and I sing your praises.

Love is the greatest gift you bring, Anointed One. I find
great reverence in worshipping accolades raised to
you. My hope is forever in you.

Deserving to live to serve your wonders is so worthy of
constant veneration. Flame of the Spirit, you make it
all possible by your sacred love.

*O God of Faith, you have blessed me endlessly. I am
trying to bring others to see and know your love.*

FEBRUARY 28

PSALM 52:8. But I am like a green olive tree in the house of God; I trust in the mercy of God for ever and ever.

Lord enthroned in heaven, you are my great Redeemer. I rejoice with exceedingly great joy for the gift of knowing you. I am jubilant at your favor.

You are the delight of angels, the exhilaration of my heart. Glory be to you, Blessed One. I acclaim your wonders. Eternal thanks for being you.

Let the earth and the seas swell in a mighty chorus of praise. Let my voice be strong among the worshipping throng. Let the hills echo the glory.

Father Confessor, I look to you as my tower of strength, and you never fail me. I offer you my loving thanks.

For Use in Leap Year

FEBRUARY 29

PSALM 47:1. O clap your hands, all ye people; shout unto God with the voice of triumph.

You, Lord, God above all gods, are wondrous beyond description. King of the earth and heavens, I extol your holiness with rich delight.

I sing out your praises, King of kings. I sing joyously for your grandeur. You are much to be praised, Jehovah. I celebrate your glorious name.

You alone are worthy of the exalted praise of all mortals. Your perfection cannot be adored enough. There is no tribute worthy of you.

Your throne will be a gathering place for songs and singers. I am praying, and trying, Lord, to join in.

MARCH 1

PSALM 119:47. And I will delight myself in thy commandments, which I have loved.

You are Lord, Jesus Christ, to the glory of the Father. Grant that I am a follower of the way of peace and love always. Let me laud you ever.

I know your lovingkindness strongly in my life, God. Your praises are always in my heart and mind. My Mighty Shepherd lives, redeems, loves.

Come hear, everyone who reveres God. He has done great things and will continue to do so. He is Jehovah, and His power and love are great.

Lord of Heavenly Hosts, may my humility be fitted to your greatness. You are so much to be revered.

MARCH 2

PSALM 31:21. Blessed be the Lord, for he hath shewed me his marvellous kindness in a strong city.

Let me carry the Good News around the world. Let people everywhere know your mercy, your love, your blessed goodness, and your power.

O God, hear your servant's prayer. Let your face shine upon me with the peace and joy only you can bring, Lord. Be my guide always.

Lord God, hear; Lord God, forgive. Lord God of Hosts Divine, eternal might is yours. There is no redemption except through Christ my King.

Most Bountiful Giver, you satisfy my every need. All good comes from you, and my prayers are answered.

MARCH 3

PSALM 24:5. He shall receive the blessing from the Lord, and righteousness from the God of his salvation.

I praise you, my Lord, for your wondrous blessings, even before they come. You are so loving and faithful that it is hard not to be expectant.

I am made right with you by faith, Father. I can have real peace only when I am proper in your sight. Christ's sacrifice put this within reach.

Make me glad all my days, Lord of Comfort, serving and praising your glory. Establish the work of my hands to your honor and eternal praise.

I acclaim you, Lord, daily and often. My hope is in you alone. You are the life I breathe.

MARCH 4

PSALM 26:12. My foot standeth in an even place; in the congregations will I bless the Lord.

Each star counted reveals two new ones. So also are my blessings and my signs of your goodness multiplied. I rejoice in you; all honor to you.

I praise you, O God of All Nations; your blessings are forever. I pray that people everywhere will join in my accolade of joyful declaration.

Let jubilant sounds echo throughout the earth. Let there be magnifying songs to your brilliance. Prince of Peace, you are exalted in my heart.

God of the years, I need only trust and believe. You have provided the sure way in love and mercy.

MARCH 5

PSALM 52:9. I will praise thee for ever, because thou hast done it; and I will wait on thy name, for it is good before the saints.

God of Love and God of Light, you speak to me through the growing fields, the hills, the rivers, the animals. You speak words of great love.

You made the earth and heavens; the universe is full of the joy you brought. Hark, my soul, there is a great wonder here. It is my Lord and Savior.

How strong and sweet your loving care really is. O Gracious One, you make a warm and sheltered place for me. You nurture me faithfully.

All-Pervasive God, my life is but a moment in your sight. Help me to live the moment prayerfully and acceptably.

MARCH 6

PSALM 95:2. Let us come before his presence with thanksgiving, and make a joyful noise unto him with psalms.

My only hope is in you, God. You will neither fail nor desert me. You are the light eternal that knows no wavering, that is the focus of my love.

It is no wonder that I am happy in you, Jesus. I have every reason to trust you, laud you, honor you, and dedicate each moment to you.

You continue forever, God of the Morning Light. You are exalted in the heavens and praised throughout the earth. I want always to be exalting you.

Great Impelling Spirit, in you I have found strength. Let me live by and love your sacred Word.

MARCH 7

PSALM 21:1. The king shall joy in thy strength, O Lord; and in thy salvation how greatly shall he rejoice.

Praise Him, all the world and its people. Praise Him mightily. Give Him thanks and adoration. Great Lord of Life, your radiance is my light.

Sing extolling songs to my Lord and God. You ride upon the clouds and command the heavens, Jehovah. You bring rich delight to my life.

In you I have found new strength, Redeemer. You have given me your sacred Word and helped me to understand it, to live by it, to love it.

I will pray always to see your majestic greatness for all eternity. I will speak only good of my Lord.

MARCH 8

PSALM 85:2. Thou hast forgiven the iniquity of thy people; thou hast covered all their sin.

Lord Most High, your glory fills the heavens. The hills echo praise, and the seas roar thunderous applause. The deep valleys hold my love.

I shout for happiness before you. I shout Hosanna to the highest heaven. All power and glory are yours, Beloved One. You are the Lord.

I obey you gladly. I come before you singing jubilantly, alive in your love. I praise you for the promise of salvation, the greatest gift.

I bow low before your feet. I revere and praise you with all the fervor at my command.

MARCH 9

PSALM 91:14. Because he hath set his love upon me, therefore will I deliver him; I will set him on high because he hath known my name.

Your Word is my delight and my counsel. Your beauty enshrines beauty, your glory encircles glory, and your brightness shines out steadily.

With the softness of dew and the sweetness of manna, God, let your Word become my hope. Your promise is my salvation and my joy.

You made the oceans, pouring into the voids from your vast reservoirs. You made all things to serve me, Lord. I am the sheep of your fold.

Author of Life, let all my boasting be of my Lord. I always know you are near, unseen but felt.

MARCH 10

PSALM 63:4. Thus will I bless thee while I live; I will lift up my hands in thy name.

I pray that your holy name will be sought more and more by all. You are mercifully supreme, Lord of All. All Hail, King of kings.

All nations, all people everywhere, praise your Redeemer Lord. His glory and majesty are eternal, and His goodness lives for us forever.

Merciful and Gracious Lord, the works of your hands include verity and judgment. To your name I offer veneration; to your Being, honor.

Blessed Lord, I am a traveler passing through the earth. Trusting ever, my time here will be for you.

MARCH 11

PSALM 18:29. For by thee I have run through a troop, and by my God I have leaped over a wall.

Praising, I will call upon you, Lord. Singing of your splendor, I will worship you. Trusting ever, I will live in you always.

I love you, God, above all things. Angels of your domain join with me in exultant chorusing. We sing together of your wonders and grace.

Blessed is the nation whose god is the Lord. Blessed are those He has chosen for His own. Blessed am I in your radiant love, Jehovah.

Let all who find you through me shout with delight. Let my voice be the most jubilant of all.

MARCH 12

PSALM 48:14. For this God is our God for ever and ever; he will be our guide even unto death.

Our sweet partnership in prayer and praise is my way of honoring and exalting your holiness. You are praise itself, glory eternal.

Thank you for the windows of grace, letting me view your greatness. My song lauds your magnificence. My hymns of homage are jubilant for you.

Praises rise to you, God, from my heart. I pray earnestly for more ways to laud and honor your holiness, to eulogize your majesty.

My worship for you, Jehovah, is for what and who you are and not for what you do for me.

MARCH 13

PSALM 132:14. This is my rest for ever; here will I dwell, for I have desired it.

Your power is greater than creation, and inconceivably mighty. My veneration is for you. Lord, your crown of glory is mine forevermore.

Great you are, Lord, and greatly to be praised. The mountain of your holiness is hallowed. You are the joy of the earth, the Lord of Hosts.

Believers rejoice in you, Blessed Lord of All. Our hearts receive rapture in your favor. God of all, true God, I worship you mightily.

Majestic Ruler, your Word guides my feet on a jeweled path. I need only to walk it faithfully.

MARCH 14

PSALM 34:22. None of them that trust in him shall be desolate.

How precious is your constant love, Lord. How favored we are to be able to acclaim your greatness and to honor your fineness.

You are the Fountain of Light. My light comes from you alone. You give unfailingly of your love to those who know you. Hallelujah, you live.

Great you are, Christ the King. You enjoy helping your children. I will tell everyone how wondrous and how splendidly magnificent you are.

Lead me as you promised, God. Tell me clearly what to do. I want to serve you and to merit your love.

MARCH 15

PSALM 25:14. The secret of the Lord is with them that fear him; and he will shew them his covenant.

Let everyone everywhere bow in reverence to my Great King. Let everyone come humbly to worship. You are mighty in all things, Jehovah.

I praise you who saved the Israelites from the power of opposing kings. They had to call upon a greater King. You daily save me from many evils.

May there be rapturous shouts of celebration to you, God above all gods. May everyone want to praise you rapturously and honor you greatly.

Your peace rules my heart; your grace is rich and divine. How great you are and how happily I worship.

MARCH 16

PSALM 81:1. Sing aloud unto God our strength; make a joyful noise unto the God of Jacob.

You shine exalted from your radiant throne. Blessed God, praised and glorified by all the hosts of heaven, I lift my voice in jubilance.

Your words are truth, Redeemer Christ. I sing my song of Galilee and of the man of the sea. All hail Christ the King. Hosanna in the highest.

I sing my celebration of your holy name. You are the sunshine after rain. Out of your Gethsemane came the legacy of peace. I adore you, Lord.

Merciful Father, let my mind be open to your teachings, and my heart to your lovingkindness.

MARCH 17

PSALM 19:7. The law of the Lord is perfect, converting the soul; the testimony of the Lord is sure, making wise the simple.

Thank you for the sweet and sacred influence of life. Lord of lords, let me balance my days between good deeds and joyful praises.

I will sing each day of your power and glory. You are my high tower of refuge, my hope, and my life. You are my song of songs, my praise.

O my Strength, to you I sing celebratory songs. You are my pinnacle of redemption, joy, and exuberant exultation. You are my radiance.

Spirit of Holiness, I confess my sins to you, and in your supreme love you forgive me and wash me clean.

MARCH 18

PSALM 85:10. Mercy and truth are met together; righteousness and peace have kissed each other.

I will magnify you, O God my King. Your praise will be on my lips forever and ever. There is no end to your greatness and no limit to your love.

Each generation will eulogize your works to another. I will talk forever of your honor and glory. Your wondrous deeds are my example.

I cannot count the times you have helped me. Your exaltation is ever on my tongue, and your deeds bring it forth often. You are life itself.

Your goodness is layered deep in the love you show the world. Let me show myself thankful.

MARCH 19

PSALM 141:8. But mine eyes are unto thee, O God the Lord; in thee is my trust, leave not my soul destitute.

You are the light of every heart, the guest of every moment. You are my Magnified Lord, Splendor Infinite and Divine. You are God.

I come to you with songs of gladness. I praise you heartily, My God and King. The earthly beauties and heavenly joy are your gifts.

You are ever gracious, Lord. You make me well in my infirmities. You comfort me and bless me. I rejoice to know you protect and love me.

Gracious King, I pray that others may know your glory and rapture. You are my greatness.

MARCH 20

PSALM 84:4. Blessed are they that dwell in thy house; they will still be praising thee.

The world's strength, joy, pleasure, happiness, and delight are enhanced daily by thoughts of you. You are my divine God of gods.

Joyful music lifts me heavenward. You are the triumphant song of life and universality. I sing my joyous songs to boost your gladsome love.

With your help, Blessed Shepherd, I pray to lead others to you. Would that others could know your glory, your rich rapture, your radiance.

Focus of my joy, you never fail to support me in all things. I am cradled in your graciousness.

MARCH 21

PSALM 17:1. Give ear to my prayer that goeth not out of feigned lips.

Lord of Life, you are my hope. My trust is in you, just as your love lasts forever. There is no faith's reward greater than you.

You have declared your glory and manifested your splendid majesty in the world. You are light eternal, praise itself, my glorification.

Your song of love sings in my heart and becomes my heavenly marching music. Let me find and keep the godly path ending at your throne.

Infinite One, let my days be worthily spent serving you. Your faithfulness is a beacon I can guide upon.

MARCH 22

PSALM 69:13. But as for me, my prayer is unto thee, O Lord, in an acceptable time; O God, in the multitude of thy mercy hear me.

Let me worship and serve you in a long life, God of Purity. Let each day added to my life be worthily spent serving you.

I look upward every day, searching for you. Knowing that you surround me completely still leaves me wanting more of your nearness.

I will sing about your lovingkindness and your justice. I will sing of your laudatory graces. I will find joy in life venerating you.

Dearest Jesus, thank you for my salvation. If you had not suffered for us, we would have been eternally doomed.

MARCH 23

PSALM 145:3. Great is the Lord, and greatly to be praised; and his greatness is unsearchable.

There is jubilation in joining others to sing eulogies to you, Triune God. Your house, Father, is made more splendid for this homage.

Let my soul praise you, Redeemer. May your saints rejoice and honor you. How good and gladsome it is to laud you, my Lord. How sweet is your Being.

Acclaim my King, servants of God everywhere. All, exalt His name. You are so gracious, God, that delighted songs are in the air everywhere.

Holy Father of our Savior, thank you. May your servants rejoice and honor you. Accept us, Lord, in your mercy.

MARCH 24

PSALM 33:11. The counsel of the Lord standeth for ever; the thoughts of his heart to all generations.

All power in heaven and earth are yours. I sing praises to your holy and blessed name. My trust is wholly in you, Beloved Master.

You alone are the wellspring of life, Father. You are the God of Ages, Patriarch. You are goodness and mercy, love, peace, and joy.

I love your name, Jesus, Immanuel, Christ the Lord. There is nowhere you are not known. Let your name be revered everywhere, lauded mightily.

Master of the Multitude, without you nothing is holy. You are my celebration. My adoration of you completes me.

MARCH 25

PSALM 97:5. The hills melted like wax at the presence of the Lord; at the presence of the Lord of the whole earth.

You will make me smile again. You are my God, my everlasting richness and jubilance. In your reflected glory I am worthy to ask forgiveness.

Rejoice in Him, all who are His or wish to be. Shout for joy, all who try to obey Him. Pay tribute to your God in revelry and celebration.

The world made beautiful at my King's command is itself praise. I sully your precious kingdom often and ask your forgiveness steadily.

God of Supremacy, all of your works are a benediction. Your love is my most enduring gift of all.

MARCH 26

PSALM 77:1. I cried unto God with my voice, and he gave ear unto me.

God of the Nations, I rejoice in living in the aura of your glory. I thank you for the life, the hope, and cheer you give. Let my deeds please you.

I extol your name, Jehovah, Lord of the Heavens. My joyful day is a day of adoration to my God. You are goodness and grace, love eternal.

This is another day you have made, Lord. Let me rejoice and be glad in it. The songs, the music, the voices strong all sing tributes to you.

I have such fullness of soul knowing you, Lord. My prayer is to find new ways to worship and praise.

MARCH 27

PSALM 22:25. My praise shall be of thee in the great congregation; I will pay my vows before them that fear him.

May everyone alive give you praise and honor you immeasurably. Lord on High, my King, you have given the world much to rejoice about.

Lord, I love to do your will. My heart's desire is to glorify your name and to bless your beloved presence. You are adoration itself.

God, your discipline is good. It leads me to life and health. I sing of your grand design, your plan of life for me. You are joy.

By trying to be nobler and more unselfish like you, let me learn how good life was intended to be.

MARCH 28

PSALM 119:90. Thy faithfulness is unto all genera-tions; thou hast established the earth and it abideth.

Faith shuts the door at night, while love opens it in the morning. My soul is honored, for it can contemplate the dazzling glories of eternity.

Sing a new song, all persons everywhere. I sing to my God in all the corners of the earth. Let the notes echo and reecho from the hills.

I sing out your praises and bless the wonder I know at being here to do so. Each day I want to tell someone you saved me, and they may also be saved by you.

Prince of Life, your divinity is powerfully manifest. You live to serve your children.

MARCH 29

PSALM 36:8. They shall be abundantly satisfied with the fatness of thy house, and thou shalt make them drink of the river of thy pleasures.

I go to the temple to praise you. I sing with exultation, delighting in your presence. I live for you and pray that I please you, Lord.

I compose my best songs to your name. My voice offers adulation to your rich glory. May everyone hear of your doings and praise you.

Your words are pure, God. You are the Word. All salvation is in you, Lord. Hear my rejoicing. Let my jubilant song reach you.

My soul is honored to understand your love for me. I am enthralled at the wonder of being your child.

MARCH 30

PSALM 146:10. The Lord shall reign for ever; even thy God, O Zion, unto all generations. Praise ye the Lord.

Lord, I praise you among all nations, great and small. I pray that everyone will join in my psalms honoring you. May the chorus be strong.

The heavens tell of your glory, God. They are a marvellous display of your craftsmanship. You alone are the worthy Almighty God.

You feed me, Blessed Lord, with blessings from your own table. You let me drink from your rivers of delight in the gayety of your presence.

Blessed Anointed One, let me crown you with many crowns. I pray the world may awaken to your splendor.

MARCH 31

PSALM 119:27. Make me to understand the way of thy precepts; so shall I talk of thy wondrous works.

You allow me to sing glad songs of jubilation to you, Precious Jehovah. I will think reverently of you and sing of your magnificence.

All glory and honor to you, the Son who set us free. With the Father and Holy Spirit we are ever one eternally. You are the standard-bearer.

Come, everyone, clap mirthfully for happiness. Shout triumphant acclaim to the Lord. Let your voices be joyous, full of ardent love for Him.

Creator of the Seasons, you have lifted me out of the pit of despair. You are the path of righteousness.

APRIL 1

PSALM 85:9. Surely his salvation is nigh them that fear him, that glory may dwell in our land.

Praise Him, my soul. All that is within me that is good praises you, God. Your holy name is revered. I never forget your goodness.

Angels who excel in strength and who possess glory, let me hear your witness for the Lord. Let me join your chorus. We can honor Him.

You ascended with glory. You will return in power and majesty so sublime the world cannot help but note. There will be many manifestations.

Divine Jehovah, your everlasting love is the safe harbor in my life. Living in you is my redemption.

APRIL 2

PSALM 78:54. And he brought them to the border of his sanctuary, even unto this mountain which his right hand had purchased.

Clap your hands lustily, everyone; sing to the Lord our God. Sing His acclaim resoundingly. Great is our Lord, manifestly holy and divine.

You are my God for always. Open my lips, O Lord, that my mouth might make glad sounds of accolades. Let the chorus swell sweetly.

O God, my Strength, let me cling to you. In you there is an abundance of love, power, goodness, and sharing. You are light and life for me.

You have given me the grace to adore you. You have given voice to the joy you bring into my heart.

APRIL 3

PSALM 144:15. Happy is that people that is in such a case; yea, happy is that people whose God is the Lord.

I will sing joyously of your magnificent splendor. I will laud you as long as I have being. May my songs please you as singing pleases me.

I applaud you, Lord of my soul. There is richness in my eulogy because you inspire it. My talk is of your wonderful works and goodness.

The mountains and hills sing; the trees and waves clap their hands joyously. The green pastures are part of your love, Blessed Shepherd.

Merciful Triune God, my hymnbook is my delight because it is of your greatness. I trust in you so.

APRIL 4

PSALM 146:5. Happy is he that hath the God of Jacob for his help, whose hope is in the Lord his God.

Teach me, your faithful servant, how to properly adore you. Fill me with your fullness now and forever. My celebration is for your presence.

I am in the midst of happiness, perfect and supreme pleasure. My heart has joy, love, hope, and wonder. Your precious glory is my light.

I exalt you for the means of grace. I pray for the seeds of truth you sowed to prosper. My Lord, Great Planter of Life, you are honor.

My constant boast is that I know of you, and I tell everyone. I will declare your fineness in all places.

APRIL 5

PSALM 105:2. Sing unto him, sing psalms unto him; talk ye of all his wondrous works.

I will praise the name of the Author of Life and Light with my gladsome song. Long and ever, I will magnify you with thanksgiving.

Let all who delight in you praise you. Let all who trust you follow you. Let all, everyone, sing of your splendor and wonder. You are my God.

I will patiently await, lauding you more and more. You are my trusted hope and my lighted path. You are lovingkindness, Lord.

King of Angels, great are your deeds, and great is my adoration. I have found myself in worshipping you.

APRIL 6

PSALM 89:2. For I have said mercy shall be built up for ever; thy faithfulness shalt thou establish in the very heavens.

All hearts and every tongue join to eulogize you. My joy is great and full of glory. I rejoice in you, Beloved Christ.

Thinking of you is a season of melting love. Revering you is my praise and glorification of you. I extol your unending wonders.

You are the hope of life, the worth of living. You are the God of all Nations, ineffably loving, infinitely divine. You are love itself.

Most High Jehovah, let me dwell in your house deservedly, having served you rightly. My holy joy is in you.

APRIL 7

PSALM 105:7. He is the Lord our God; his judgments are in all the earth.

Glory in the Lord, all people of the earth. O worshippers of God, rejoice. Heaven and earth are full of His glory, and He is available to us.

You are my Lord, my God Omnipresent. Your goodness and grace are seen in many things. You are the King; power and majesty flow from you.

You are so great, Lord God. You are higher than the heavens and the stars you put in place. You live, God, and your love is all-enveloping.

There is nowhere your wisdom is not found. In your plan I need no other salvation.

APRIL 8

PSALM 145:2. Every day will I bless thee, and I will praise thy name for ever and ever.

Forever singing as I shine, the hand that made me is divine. O Infinite Jehovah, you are magnificently splendid, inexpressibly wondrous.

You fill my mouth with laughter and you give my lips exultant shouts of joy. You make the darkness bright, and all the world is alive.

By your knowledge the depths are broken up and the clouds drop down the dew. I bow before your greatness and adore your presence.

God of the Morning Light, I ask your forgiveness. I praise you immediately, for I know you will respond.

APRIL 9

PSALM 33:2. Praise the Lord with harp; sing unto him with the psaltery and an instrument of ten strings.

I offer glory to you, Beloved Lord, high in the heavens. I greet you with a blessing and my praise. I honor and magnify your presence.

May all esteem be given to you always, Jesus my Redeemer. You came to save me. You showed me the Way. I pray that I am listening fully.

Lord of Life, exalted above the high heavens, receive my adulation. Show the world your great glory that all may honor you.

You are all that is good and great and true. Each day is newer and brighter than the last you made.

APRIL 10

PSALM 37:5. Commit thy way unto the Lord; trust also in him and he shall bring it to pass.

My Father in heaven, you make the lilies grow, the ravens fly, the rivers flow, and the seeds to grow. Your glory is evident everywhere.

I sing mirthful songs to you, Most High Jehovah. You have made me glad through your works, your love, your redemptive sacrifice.

Venerate my Lord, O my soul. All that is within me that is good, laud His glorious Being. Majestic Universal Lord, I worship you.

Matchless King, long ago in sacred silence you died that I might live. I pray my life will make me worthy.

APRIL 11

PSALM 40:3. And he hath put a new song in my mouth, even praise unto our God; many shall see it, and fear, and shall trust in the Lord.

I worship you, Lord God, in the beauty of your holiness. The world is awestruck at your wonders. Glory be to you on high, my Savior King.

Your kindness and your power of creation surround me. You supply my every need until I dwell with you above. I am trying to merit a place.

Blessed are you on the exalted throne of your kingdom. I will praise and magnify you forever, Great Spirit. I sing exultant songs to you.

Soul of my days, the galaxies that soar to infinity are yours. Let me prepare to see your face, Lord God.

APRIL 12

PSALM 119:72. The law of thy mouth is better to me than thousands of gold and silver.

You give such goodness, God of the Precious Word. Everything I have is from you. My prayer is that I may love and obey your Word.

Love sings and shines forever through you. Its praise is for my Lord. My joy is in the hope of oneness with you, oneness I can now win.

You created it all, God of Strength. All power, glory, and honor are yours. It was for your glory that creation came about. May I keep it so.

Infinitely Wise Father, I can trust in you always. My faith will be steady because I have you.

APRIL 13

PSALM 17:15. As for me, I will behold thy face in righteousness; I shall be satisfied, when I awake, with thy likeness.

Sanctify me, Lord. Let my voice soar to the heavens to find affinity with the angelic choruses praising you. All hail Savior Mine.

Let the nations rejoice and be glad in you. You bless us, though all the ends of the earth fear you. My soul is in your eternal keeping.

I worship Him with you, angels of heaven. He is my praiseworthy King also, my Lord of Life. I speak only good of my Redeemer.

Crown of Graciousness, let me enjoy your fatherly goodness forever. I tremble before you in my love.

APRIL 14

PSALM 81:2. Take a psalm, and bring hither the timbrel, the pleasant harp with the psaltery.

You will come in majesty, with your angels surrounding you. You will sit upon a throne of glory to judge the living and the dead.

Eternal Lord, you are the God Majestic. You are a great God all can eulogize. It is joyous and pleasant to laud you with great merriment.

Your throne, Almighty Giver of Every Good, is forever and ever. Your scepter of righteousness is my guide. I worship your glorious Being.

You came, Lord, to ransom souls and to be loved in return. There are many of us worshipping and praising.

APRIL 15

PSALM 81:10. I am the Lord thy God, which brought thee out of the land of Egypt; open thy mouth wide, and I will fill it.

Your crown of glory is magnificent, God. Your name is exceedingly excellent. In all the world there is eternal praise to be given, Blessed Master.

I hear the glad sounds; my Savior is coming. He is the Savior promised to return to earth. Everyone, everywhere, rejoice. He comes.

I pray every heart may prepare a throne for you, Redeemer. I pray every voice may be attuned to glory as it lifts psalms of praise to you.

O Blessed Comforter, your commandments are pure and they gladden my heart. I pray to be constant and good.

APRIL 16

PSALM 135:5. For I know that our Lord is great, and that our Lord is above all gods.

Awake, my soul, I sing to my Lord who died for me. I hail my Lord as my Matchless King. Through all eternity He is supreme. All hail.

No angels in the sky can leave a song unsung when it is able to praise you. You are the Christ King I pay homage to. You are my redemptive Lord.

Be ever near me Christ, my Lord and Savior. Be my joy throughout each day. Let me praise you with a gladsome heart, with a joyous song.

Your helping hand is always outstretched. Your love is my continuing hope. I gladly pay homage to you.

APRIL 17

PSALM 34:22. The Lord redeemeth the soul of his servants.

Let your kingdom come. Let your scepter and crown bring blessings innumerable. Let your salvation save. Let me forever sing psalms to you.

All the faithful everywhere, come in joy and triumph. Come to Bethlehem in spirit, to worship our King. Come to behold and praise Him.

Precious gifts brought to you are received in the same way as the widow's mite. Adoration, trust, and praise are still the better gifts.

All things were written to teach me, Blessed Monarch. Your Scriptures bring a sweet message of love.

APRIL 18

PSALM 86:6. Give ear, O Lord, unto my prayer; and attend to the voice of my supplications.

I pray all nations may know and profess it is my Lord who reigns supreme. He constantly watches over all of us with love.

Salvation belongs to you, Lord God. Your blessing is in offering it to me. I have been given a way to your throne and I acclaim you.

May the vast seas roar, and the countryside and everything in it rejoice. You are the Savior I treasure; you are my King of kings.

Blameless Lord, prepare my heart and cleanse my soul for your coming. You came, died, left, and will return.

APRIL 19

PSALM 57:7. My heart is fixed, O God; I will sing and give praise.

I praise you, my God, in all your noble acts. I praise you according to your exceeding goodness. I pray that all with breath may praise.

I pray you will be lauded with lute and harp, in the timbrels and dances, upon the strings and pipes and loud cymbals. You live.

Angels of heaven, come with wings unfurled singing glad songs and bringing tribute. I rejoice that I may join in your singing from where I am.

I come to your side, trustingly, and I am not wrong. I sing psalms and hymns to your Magnificence.

APRIL 20

PSALM 89:5. And the heavens shall praise thy wonders, O Lord; thy faithfulness also in the congregation of the saints.

I sing glad songs to you, Lord. You have done wonders for me. I will make known your esteem throughout the world. You are so praiseworthy.

I hear people singing to you from the ends of the earth. They sing of the splendor of the Righteous One, my Lord, my Redeemer.

I worship you, Lord God Almighty. I offer my prayers and my praise to your majesty and greatness. My tributes are for you alone.

Perfect Being, Eden's door stands wide at your wish. You are greatly to be honored, and I wish to excel.

APRIL 21

PSALM 98:5. Sing unto the Lord with the harp; with the harp, and the voice of a psalm.

I honor you, God, for your Eternal Word. My trust is always in you. I rejoice in my knowledge of you. Awake, my glory, honor Him.

I sing to you, Wise and Loving Father. There is no greater gift than your love. No praise is jubilant enough to honor you properly.

Joy, joy, my Lord is always nigh. You live in every living thing. You are so available, so readily at hand to adore, so worthy to worship.

I will bring everyone to worship you. I will tell of your wonders and brilliance. I will speak of my love.

APRIL 22

PSALM 84:11. For the Lord is a sun and shield; the Lord will give grace and glory; no good thing will he withhold from them that walk uprightly.

Angels of heaven accompany their joyous songs with harp and lyre. It is a mighty chorus of adulation to my King. There is no one worthier.

I praise you, my Lord, and give you honor for all the mighty things you continuously do. You are always near, denoting my measure of love.

I exalt you, Glorious God. You purchased me and guaranteed that I could find my way to you. You have preserved me for eternity.

Wondrous God, the world had a new beginning in you.
I received hope and pray to use this chance wisely.

APRIL 23

PSALM 89:17. For thou art the glory of their strength, and in thy favor our horn shall be exalted.

I make glad sounds to you. I serve you with gladness, Gracious and Divine Lord. I sing to my Soul of Souls with great celebration.

Dwell in me. Never leave me, though I am a sinner and unworthy of you. Vast riches are mine when you are a guest in my heart.

Let the righteous be glad. Let all rejoice before you, Lord God on High. Let everyone be merry and joyfully laud you. You are life and love.

Magnificent Presence, you have shown me how to perfectly love. Your example will be my guiding light.

APRIL 24

PSALM 16:11. Thou wilt shew me the path of life; in thy presence is fulness of joy; at thy right hand there are pleasures for evermore.

My voice raises gladly in exultant songs of thanks to you. I sing hallelujah with the angels. All hail, Christ the King is with me.

May my song be as rich, full, and free as the bird's. May my love for you show through my praising words. Let my love be fulsome.

My hope, belief, and trust are in you. My pleasure and happiness come in acclaiming your greatness. Give me the ability to wonder.

Thank you for your endless care. I adore your greatness surrounding me. You are my priceless privilege.

APRIL 25

PSALM 86:4. Rejoice the soul of the servant; for unto thee, O Lord, do I lift up my soul.

God in Three Persons, Blessed Trinity, you are comprehensible through faith. I have no reason not to love you and praise you greatly.

The flowers of the garden, bees sipping honey, birds nesting; all are praise to you. Singing joyfully is not the only accolade.

I offer you glad worship and veneration, Lord. You are my sacred Redeemer, my life's ransom. You are my joyful and wondrous inheritance.

Your wisdom and great knowledge lift me, Lord of Splendor. You are to be given great adulation.

APRIL 26

PSALM 92:1. It is a good thing to give thanks unto the Lord, and to sing praises unto thy name, O most High.

You are the light of my morning, stabilizer of my days, wonder of my life. The more known you are, the more lauded and loved you are.

Let me fall at your feet, adoring. Let me join in the everlasting song. Let me crown you Ruler. Hear my acclaim; all glory to you, Jehovah.

O for a thousand tongues to sing and extol you, Great and Precious Lord. Let me sing of your glory, your redemptive sacrifice, your greatness.

O Holy One, your might is mine to speak about. Your holy name is mine to praise before others.

APRIL 27

PSALM 139:14. I will praise thee for I am fearfully and wonderfully made; marvellous are thy works, and that my soul knoweth right well.

May the princes of the people gather together to honor my Lord. You are on your throne of holiness, God, and you rule eternally.

You are my holy place of refuge. You are my eternal fortress. I trust in you completely, Lord, and I know your strength is mine to share.

Love the Lord, all, including His saints and angels. You have preserved the faithful and you reward those who revere you. You are my reward.

I am glad in you, Great and Brilliant God. Your Word is immortal, your goodness eternal.

APRIL 28

PSALM 149:6. Let the high praises of God be in their mouth, and a two-edged sword in their hand.

You are the great and mighty Lord, God above all. You have all wisdom, and you perform mighty miracles. There is no limit to your power.

You have made your name very great, as it is now and forever. Your words and works are magnificent. Your love is a constant, my hope.

I am glad in you, my Lord. I rejoice to know your wondrous favor. I shout joyously in agreement with you. You are the Lord God.

You are the source of my joy, hope, trust, faith. I worship at your exalted throne, Jehovah.

APRIL 29

PSALM 105:1. O give thanks unto the Lord, call upon his name; make known his deeds among the people.

I will sing to you, God, as long as I live. I will praise you with my last breath. I pray my life may be lived so that I can do this.

I declare your wonders and your works the amazement of the age. I worship at your exalted throne and I joyfully know your splendor.

Sing aloud unto God, all. Make a joyful noise to the God of Jacob. Let your hearts be filled with jubilation in His sight.

Epitome of Brilliance, you alone blow away my sins. You open a way through the waters and guide me always.

APRIL 30

PSALM 124:8. Our help is in the name of the Lord, who made heaven and earth.

Heaven and earth are filled with your glory. My life is enriched by accepting you as my Lord and Savior. The earth waited long for you.

Sing praises, O sea. Sing, all who live in lands beyond the sea. Sing, sing high praises to Him. He is the Lord.

You poured out your joy on humankind. It is my resolve to return enough love to increase your joy. It can be an endless circle of love.

I am content in you, All-Knowing Father. Your love is the sum total of my needs. I desire only to please.

MAY 1

PSALM 77:15. Thou hast with thine arm redeemed thy people, the sons of Jacob and Joseph.

Lord, you are my King. I want to serve you. Glory to you in the highest heaven, Jehovah. You bring peace and delight to those who serve.

As I age, Lord, teach me to know more of you. Let me appreciate your great gifts. Let me know and love your wonder for its greatness.

Book of love, of grace, of glory; gifts from my Gracious God. Wondrous is your sacred story, bright with truth and love everlasting.

Comforter of All, what joy is mine to praise and honor you. It is good giving you thanks, appreciating you.

MAY 2

PSALM 26:8. Lord, I have loved the habitation of thy house, and the place where thine honour dwelleth.

To you whose unfathomed love in beauty flows, who shaped the rose, who created snow, my thanks. You are miraculous in all you do.

The wonder of your name evokes an exultant song. The beauty of your being is a call to love. Your lovingkindness is forever, Lord.

Grant me your Spirit, Master of my Days. Enrich me with your radiance. I crown you with adoration, Lord of the Legions. I worship you.

O Mighty Potter, mold me to your liking. You are gloriously God, and it is my honor to pray before you.

MAY 3

PSALM 33:5. He loveth righteousness and judgment; the earth is full of the goodness of the Lord.

In your temple all are praising you. Glory, glory, glory to my Lord on high. Hallelujah. You are the Majestic Jehovah who lives.

I praise you lovingly, God. You refuse always to let my enemies triumph, and you show me the way to turn them away. I am trying to return love.

Sing to Him, saints above, sing and give thanks to His greatness. Sing loud and laudatory eulogies to my God; glorify the Blessed One.

I have the knowledge and the will to worship, and I have a God of Grandeur for my Lord. I desire no one else.

MAY 4

PSALM 19:6. His going forth is from the end of the heaven, and his circuit unto the ends of it; and there is nothing hid from the heat thereof.

You are my Blessed Rock. I cry out my praises to your glory. I am saved in joyous communion with you, Blessed Master.

The brilliance of your presence breaks through the clouds in lightning. You are eternally the Lord Most High. I want to merit your love.

Anoint the prophets. Men who will hear, share. Let the prophets awake to human needs, and intercede where it is your will.

Shield and Comforter, I stand secure in the circle of your love. I can stand against sin in your name.

MAY 5

PSALM 3:3. But thou, O Lord, art a shield for me; my glory, and the lifter up of mine head.

Everyone who does right comes gladly to you, God. Your light lets us see to do what pleases you. We praise you, God; we revere you mightily.

When the flood passes and I am still among those left, Lord, let me begin immediately to laud your name. You are joy and hope eternal.

I have benefitted so from the rich blessings you brought the world, Jesus. You have heaped blessings upon blessings on me, Lord.

There is no limit to your power and love, God. May I never cease to search for righteousness.

MAY 6

PSALM 71:23. My lips shall greatly rejoice when I sing unto thee, and my soul, which thou hast redeemed.

Praise Him, heaven and earth. All inhabitants everywhere have knowledge of you. Everyone knows you as the King, the Father Almighty.

I praise you along with the stars and the seas you created. I praise your glorious deeds and live reverently in your light. I want to serve.

I sing a new song to my Father Supreme. You are everything in my life, Lord God. I learn new reasons daily to acclaim your greatness.

Your lovingkindness is great beyond measure, and your goodness pervades my life. Thank you for hope and love.

MAY 7

PSALM 17:8. Keep me as the apple of the eye; hide me under the shadow of thy wings.

Give acclaim to my Lord, all. My eyes lift up to behold your glory, yet I fear your dazzling splendor. Voices join my devotional song.

Holy, holy, holy, Lord of Hosts. The world is full of your fineness. My veneration for your greatness and wonder is for always.

I lift up my soul to you, God of Jubilation. I trust in you completely. I have no cause, ever, to doubt you, Redeemer. You are wondrous.

I will tell about your wondrous works. Add new miracles, Lord, so that I may also praise them.

MAY 8

PSALM 79:9. Help us, O God of our salvation, for the glory of thy name; and deliver us, and purge away our sins, for thy name's sake.

Glory to you, Father, Son, and Holy Spirit. Your name is Trinity, glory for all. Your lovingkindness is legendary.

Beloved Spirit, you are blessed. Lord God of Israel, you will reign forever. I pray everyone will give you proper thanks and love.

Tell the people of the world of His mighty miracles, which still live in today's life. Sing to Him, sing His praise. He is Divine.

Eternal God, let me see the brightness beyond the stars. Your gift of deliverance lets me dream.

MAY 9

PSALM 95:1. O come, let us sing unto the Lord; let us make a joyful noise to the rock of our salvation.

You are the light of my morning. You are a cloudless sunrise, and the refreshment after rain. You bring deliverance, your greatest gift.

Let me see the eternal brightness on the other side, Lord. Let me serve and have your rich reward. Let me luxuriate in your radiance.

Your wisdom, love, and power bind me to you, O Gracious Father. Renew a right spirit within me and let me live exultantly in you.

Font of Divinity, you are beloved in all ways. I believe and trust you and I will see you face-to-face.

MAY 10

PSALM 90:14. O satisfy us early with thy mercy, that we may rejoice and be glad all our days.

The light of heaven shines upon me in continuous love. Lord of Hosts, help me to deserve your wonderful assistance and blessed love.

May the devout increase in godly zeal. Let praise be more loudly sung to my Lord. Let men and angels shout joyously and gloriously.

I wait for your word of peace, Christ my Redeemer. You are my glory and my light. My hope and joy are in you. I need no other strength.

Lord of Perpetual Light, you give me many ways to earn my way. The path to glory is open.

MAY 11

PSALM 145:11. They shall speak of the glory of thy kingdom, and talk of thy power.

Let me be in you forever, my Gracious Lord and Savior. May I never forsake you or disappoint you. I want to live a blessed life in your sight.

You are the God of my jubilation and exultation. You are my Comforter, my Redeemer, my Eternal Father. All hail, Lord of Salvation.

I praise you, God, with an outpouring of my soul and with all my being. I eulogize your name and its goodness and greatness.

You created light. The sun and stars function as you ordained. Still, Lord, you let me join you.

MAY 12

PSALM 105:43. And he brought forth his people with joy, and his chosen with gladness.

I think about the kindnesses you show me, God. I bless your praiseworthy goodness and I will strive to merit it. I love you, Lord.

O God of Beauty, my heart is happy to extol your wonders. I will sing and rejoice before you. I will sing of your omnipresent glories.

My faithful Savior, you have made it possible for me to share your kingdom. I need only trust, believe, and love. Guide me, Holy Spirit.

King of Glory, you made the world wonderful, yet it pales at the hope of seeing your throne.

MAY 13

PSALM 86:16. Give thy strength unto thy servant and save the son of thy handmaid.

Jehovah, you created the heavens and earth and put everything in place to operate eternally. You made my world a wonderful place.

Sing for joy, O heavens. O earth, break forth in joyous song. The Lord comforts His people, and we can praise Him resoundingly.

All hail the power of Jesus' name. Let angels sing your praises. God, bring forth the crown that I may adorn my Lord and Savior.

I pray to always be among the faithful. I know the Way and I am trying to follow it always.

MAY 14

PSALM 105:5. Remember his marvellous works that he hath done, his wonders, and the judgments of his mouth.

Heaven holds so many wonderful songs that mortal ear cannot comprehend. May I eulogize you to the best of my mortal ability.

Lord, you are the only true God. You are the Living God. You are the Everlasting King whose Spirit is with me always.

You are merciful, Redeemer Lord. I will wait on you and keep to your Way. I will exalt your holy name in joyous tidings of rich rapture.

You gird me with strength, God of Israel. You are life and love. Your gentleness has made me more fitting.

MAY 15

PSALM 145:10. All thy works shall praise thee, O Lord, and thy saints shall bless thee.

I praise you mightily and joyously, God, Father of my Lord Jesus Christ. You have blessed me with greatness because I belong to Christ.

All acclaim is due you, Lord of Eternity, for your favor. You great kindnesses to me are beyond valuation. You love me and I am complete.

To know you is to see the holy vision. To love you is to find a return compellingly sweet, fully delightful, and supremely joyous.

Eternal Goodness, I praise and adore you. I pray that everyone will honor you with a good life.

MAY 16

PSALM 43:4. Then I will go unto the altar of God, unto God my exceeding joy; yea, upon the harp will I praise thee, O God my God.

Spirit of the blessed Holy Spirit, receive my celebratory rejoicing. Your living waters flow with soul-refreshing streams.

Glory to you, Lord, forever and ever. Let the world sing out laudatory songs of love and joy. Hallelujah to the great King of kings.

You agreed that all who believe and are baptized will see your salvation. I am one of those comforted in baptism, God, and supremely happy.

My soul thirsts for you, Precious Redeemer. I have been invited to follow and my heart is very joyous.

MAY 17

PSALM 81:8. Hear, O my people, and I will testify unto thee, O Israel, if thou wilt hearken unto me.

In your blessed light I am informed and strong, my Lord Jesus. In your reflected glory I can trod your path. In you I am loved.

Behold, Lord, your eye is on those who fear you, and those who hope in your mercy. You are just, Lord, and my hope in you is strong.

I have been young, and now I age. In all, I have never seen the godly forsaken. You are love, and you blanket all with your loving goodness.

Master Planner, you are the same perfection endlessly. I am prostrate at your altar, worshipping you.

MAY 18

PSALM 25:6. Remember, O Lord, thy tender mercies and thy lovingkindness; for they have been ever of old.

Sing to the Lord, O kingdoms everywhere. Sing His praises far and wide. Acclaim Him, revere Him, and extol His blessed name forever.

I will eulogize you, God, with my joyful singing. My reverent thanks go with my rejoicing. My ecstasy is in being allowed to praise.

I lift my hands in prayer and my eyes worship you. God of Consolation, I raise my voice in adulation, as I tell the world of your wonders.

Heaven and earth are a manifestation of your greatness. There is one God before me; I need no other.

MAY 19

PSALM 31:16. Make thy face to shine upon thy servant; save me for thy mercies' sake.

Your glory can be hidden from eyes blinded by sin. Forgiveness removes the veil and adoration can follow. Sinners, rejoice; He is here.

I worship you who made the heavens and the earth. Your creation is the outpouring of your greatness. Only your supreme love is greater.

Great and marvelous are your doings, Lord God Almighty. Your ways are just and true, O King of Ages. I praise your holy name.

Your glory is everywhere, God, perfectly surrounding me. There is no joy greater than adoring you.

MAY 20

PSALM 145:7. They shall abundantly utter the memory of thy great goodness, and shall sing of thy righteousness.

You are Christ, the Messiah, Son of the living God. You alone are truly good, truly wondrous, truly holy. Hosanna, you live.

Praise you, Lord God. Let all the people of the earth, rich and poor, join in the celebration. Let everyone rejoice and be jubilant.

You are my blessed King of old. You are salvation in the midst of the earth. You are the Divine Master, the Prince of Peace.

Great Lord of Life, I am blessed because you chose to bless me, to allow me to approach your glory.

MAY 21

PSALM 89:1. I will sing of the mercies of the Lord for ever; with my mouth will I make known my faith to all generations.

You, the Messiah, are the Master of even the Sabbath. You are the delight of the world, Teacher, Blessed Shepherd. You are the Lord.

You shine out of Zion, Lord. You are the perfection of beauty. You reign in splendor and magnificent power. You are divinity.

Glory and honor to you forever, Blessed One. You are the King of kings, God Almighty. You are the unseen one who never dies, Eternal Lord.

Magnified Lord, your truths shine brightly. You created truth, honor, greatness. I pray to be like you.

MAY 22

PSALM 78:72. So he fed them by the integrity of his heart, and guided them by the skilfulness of his hands.

You have given me a new song to sing. It is a song of praising magnification to my Lord. You are a richly radiant song of joy.

Many can now be heard singing your glories, Lord God. All can join in my adulation. All hail; all persons do homage to our Savior.

Let me journey to you, Fountain of Light. Let me see the magnitude and wonders of your home. Let me be part of your angelic chorus.

You gave me great abilities if I will but use them. I will do so in your service, Lord of Might.

MAY 23

PSALM 51:15. O Lord, open thou my lips and my mouth shall shew forth thy praise.

All, go through His gates with great thanksgiving. Enter His courts with songs praising the Great Spirit, my God. Sing exultantly.

O Lord God of heaven and the entire earth, exaltation is deservedly yours. You give so much. I have only love to bring and I do so, Lord.

A happy home is one where you are loved the dearest, and a willing heart is one that lives for you. A joyous tongue lauds you ceaselessly.

I will post the glad tidings everywhere. You are the true light. You are mine, Lord, and I am yours.

MAY 24

PSALM 87:1. His foundation is in the holy mountains.

Your kingdom stretches from shore to shore. My magnification is intended to crown you with glory. Blessings abound wherever you are.

You are the glory of all people, Blessed Author of Life. Your greatness is unequalled. My delight in you is unending.

My joy in the endless wonder of having you near is my celebration. Let insight increase my pleasure; let knowledge give me new praises.

Immaculate Heart, you alone are divine and unequalled. You have shown me boundless grace. I adore you.

MAY 25

PSALM 40:11. Withhold not thou thy tender mercies from me, O Lord; let thy lovingkindness and thy truth continually preserve me.

You have made your people strong. They can honor you mightily and gloriously in a never-ending chorus. They can shout jubilantly about you.

Let us sing a new song, a song of everlasting peace. Let the hills resound with the delighted rejoicing that finds voice in me.

I am happy with my heart, my voice, my soul. My joy is unconfined because you are so worthy. I pray for the right to stand before you, Lord.

My heart rejoices and I trust in your holy name. I will praise you publicly and acclaim you.

MAY 26

PSALM 89:8. O Lord God of hosts, who is a strong Lord like unto thee, or to thy faithfulness round about thee.

Let the things I do please you. Let my life be pure in your sight. Let me come to your eternal joy with ringing praise and thanksgiving.

Let me sing to you, Lord. Let my jubilant songs echo in your holy hill. You are the Great King above all notables. You are the Almighty Father.

You called me to the true faith, Lord God. Hallelujah. My greatest earthly joy was realized. I am bathed in the goodness of belief, the balm of love.

Mighty Jehovah, you showed me how to distinguish right from wrong. I will try to live in rightness.

MAY 27

PSALM 135:20. Bless the Lord, O house of Levi; ye that fear the Lord, bless the Lord.

The heavens declare your majestic glory. Most Gracious God, the firmament is but a very small part of your marvelous handiwork.

Lead me to your holy hill, Good Shepherd. God of my joy and gladness, your gifts are beyond understanding. I can only worship silently.

You are the King of kings, Light Forever. My heart overflows with love, and my voice lifts in praise to you. Your Way is perfect, God.

King of the Universe, you are eternally magnificent. My heart is quiet and confident in you.

MAY 28

PSALM 79:13. So we thy people and sheep of thy pasture will give thee thanks for ever; we will shew forth thy praise to all generations.

There is a song in the air, a bird in the sky, a prayer, a cry. The world has a King, a King sublime in power, enriched in abiding love.

There is a tumult of joy in me. I echo the songs of honor to you which come from the angelic chorus. The songs sweep over the earth.

The herald angels sang, "Glory to the newborn King." All hail the Son of Righteousness. You gave meaning and love to my life.

Your goodness reshaped the world and rules my life. You live, and my life is worthwhile.

MAY 29

PSALM 69:16. Hear me, O Lord, for thy lovingkindness is good; turn unto me according to the multitude of thy tender mercies.

Eternal Source of Love, I rejoice that there are no bounds to your goodness. You give of your wonders richly. May my praise return some measure.

I find pleasure and gladness in each new day you mold. Sharing in your perfect life is cause to sing, and I sing joyously to you.

I sing of you, Lord, for you deal with me so lovingly. Your holy hills echo and reecho my loving acclaim to you, Jehovah.

Lord of Supreme Knowledge, the joy of your countenance is mine to know. We need only love one another.

MAY 30

PSALM 111:3. His work is honourable and glorious; and his righteousness endureth for ever.

Exceedingly glad I am that your salvation came. You give me my heart's desire in all you do and in all you are. I am blessed in your goodness.

You make me radiantly happy with the joy of your countenance. You are my Exalted Savior. I sing to laud your greatness, your fineness.

Revere Him, all. He is your Lord. He alone is God, forever and ever. He reigns in heaven and earth. He is Truth, the Way, the Word.

God of gods, my hymns are earnest and exultantly jubilant. My prayer is my declaration of love.

MAY 31

PSALM 111:4. He hath made his wonderful works to be remembered; the Lord is gracious and full of compassion.

The highest bliss of heaven and earth is to praise you, Lord. Great Creator of the Powerful Word, I lift my voice to you in rapture.

Your light is mine through the grace, doctrine, and miracles of Jesus. Your goodness and mercy are incalculable; your worth is infinite.

O Eternal Word of Heavenly Promise, thank you for your greatness ever and always. Grant me, Light of the World, to walk in your splendor.

King of kings, I behold your glory all around me. I have faith and I fully trust in your word.

JUNE 1

PSALM 139:17. How precious are thy thoughts unto me, O God; how great is the sum of them.

Lord, raise up your power and come among us. Your bounteous grace and infinite mercy are everywhere. Come, all, adore Him. He is the King.

To you, God of the Morning Light, let there be glory and honor. I rejoice just to know you and your graciousness, Lord.

You rule the oceans when the winds make them angry. You make the waves subside. You are power and might, and the absolute of all wisdom.

I offer acclaim and tribute to the Lord of my heart. I pray for my celestial meeting with you, Jesus.

JUNE 2

PSALM 35:27. Let them shout for joy and be glad; yea, let them say continuously that the Lord is magnified, which has pleasure in the prosperity of his servant.

Hosanna I sing, and you listen lovingly. You rejoice for the hymns of love and adoration. I sing only to my Lord, whom I love.

Joyfully, joyfully, I adore you, God of Glory and Lord of Love. Earth and heaven reflect your rays. You are exaltation itself.

Angels sing all around your throne. You are the center of unbroken praise. You are the wellspring of the abundant joy of living.

Supreme Savior, your mighty power is used so mercifully. My hands and my prayers lift up to you.

JUNE 3

PSALM 91:11. For he shall give his angels charge over thee, to keep thee in all thy ways.

All the earth worships you, God of the Universe. Some persons are not yet praising you; they need release of their love.

Jehovah, you are the great King, above all gods. I worship you. I kneel before you. You are my God Divine. You are my miracle.

God, Father of Life, Friend, you love me and all mankind. You love first and best, wanting our love but not commanding it. You are my joy.

King of the earth, your glory is revealed as I pray to you. I thank you for all my blessings.

JUNE 4

PSALM 21:6. For thou hast made him most blessed for ever; thou hast made him exceedingly glad with thy countenance.

Jehovah, Lord of Hosts, you are the King of glory. You are strong and mighty. I adore you and I sing songs to your majesty and brilliance.

All who love the Lord, praise and honor Him. Before the God of my life, I am offering accolades of joy. You are my chosen path, Jehovah.

Would that I had the accompaniment of harps and lyres to add to my songs of eulogy. You are graciousness and fineness, and much to be praised.

Jesus Redeemer, I worship you with my heart and soul. My heart was fashioned to hold love for you.

JUNE 5

PSALM 16:8. I have set the Lord always before me; because he is at my right hand I shall not be moved.

O All-Persuasive God, you speak to the souls of all. Give me the glory of love that lasts, hopes that do not fade. Let me abide in you.

There is a special joy in knowing you, Lord. There is an even greater joy in living to please you, praise you, revere you.

Lighten my dark clouds; defend me from peril. God, direct my doings and hearken to my psalms of glory fashioned to acclaim your greatness.

Great Counsellor, let the earth ring delightedly with tributes to you. Hear my voice joining in.

JUNE 6

PSALM 119:164. Seven times a day do I praise thee, because of thy righteous judgments.

Praise the Lord, all of you. Let everyone pay homage to Him. Let the earth ring delightedly with the tributes offered to your name.

Let me sing to you, God of the Multitudes. Let me rejoice in the glory of your salvation. Let me come before you in awe, praising.

Praise be to you, Holy Spirit. You pray for me with such fervor that I am blessed continuously. My words are meager to express my joy.

Fountain of Radiance, I come to your temple often to laud and worship you. I have other kneeling places.

JUNE 7

PSALM 135:19. Bless the Lord, O house of Israel; bless the Lord, O house of Aaron.

There is a tumult of joy over the earth. The stars rain fire, the world sings. Hallelujah. Bethlehem provided the world with a King.

You are my God on high. I live to see your love revealed. Glory to you, Lamb of God. You and yours are glory and honor. I live to love you.

Your works of love and friendship are all around me. I give you my thoughts, my hopes, my heart. I will cleanse them to make them acceptable.

Focus of my prayers, nothing of any goodness compares to you. You are incomparable and mine.

JUNE 8

PSALM 29:2. Give unto the Lord the glory due his name.

Grant me true repentance and your Holy Spirit. Let me please you. Let me live to laud your greatness, honoring your holy name.

Jehovah, you are wondrous magnificence. You are the Comforter and Savior my heart desires. I call upon you often. I praise you as often.

Give grace, Heavenly Father, give grace to live righteously for you. Let me honor you by my deeds and laud you with my mouth.

I know and travel all the ways to your glorious presence. Let me continue my faith and trust.

JUNE 9

PSALM 104:35. Let the sinners be consumed out of the earth; bless thou the Lord, O my soul, praise ye the Lord.

You are the King of glory, Lord. O Christ, you are the everlasting Son of the Father. Day by day, I laud you more and more.

I proclaim your greatness, God. Everything you do is just and fair. I sing my praises to your holy name. My worship is for you alone.

How I rejoice, for no one is as holy as you, Lord. There is no God, no Rock, no Redeemer, no Lord such as you. My celebration is in you.

All-Powerful Lord, you are more to be desired than gold, more sweet than honey, more pure than purity.

JUNE 10

PSALM 148:13. Let them praise the name of the Lord, for his name alone is excellent; his glory is above the earth and heaven.

What a glorious Lord you are. You take on my burdens and give me only love. My pleasure is to return your love and to serve you.

Let the words of my mouth, and my meditations, venerate your holy name. You are the strength of my body, the fiber of my being.

Lord, I am coming to you. I want mightily to please you with my deeds. Let your strength support me and your guidance lead me to you.

Superior Being, grant me humility and penance. My pride and arrogance are sinful. I pray for new strength.

JUNE 11

PSALM 145:12. Make known to the sons of men his mighty acts, and the glorious majesty of his kingdom.

I have lifted my soul, my Lord God, to seek you. Let me walk honestly and prayerfully in your sight, extolling your goodness and greatness.

I pray everything everywhere will praise you, Lord. I worship and revere you and want all to join in. What a joy it is to serve.

The brightness of your glory, O Mighty Potter, is forever reflected for me. You anoint me with gladness. You make my heart swell with acclaim.

Shaper of Destiny, let your peace work surely in my heart. I will wash my hands in your innocence.

JUNE 12

PSALM 34:1. I will bless the Lord at all times; his praise shall continually be in my mouth.

I rejoice in you exceedingly, Lord, for always. Let your peace be mine. Let me continuously know the pure joy of your love.

Your mercy, Jehovah, is extremely great. Forgiven, I am beautiful with radiant grace. Why would I not sing to your great distinction.

I will sing to you, Lord, for you have triumphed splendidly. You are my song, my strength, my salvation. In you I am blessedly redeemed.

Christ, my Lord, I fear no unfairness of judgment. I pray to be within the range of salvation.

JUNE 13

PSALM 111:1. Praise ye the Lord; I will praise the Lord with my whole heart, in the assembly of the upright and in the congregation.

Let everyone sing a song of thanksgiving and tell of your magnificent miracles. Let everyone extol your greatness in song and story.

I publicly praise you, God. You continuously bring me back from sinful excursions. You never fail to rescue me, though I continuously fail.

Your honor is great in the sight of the world. I am glad before the beauty of your countenance. I bring you my tribute and celebrate your merit.

Almighty God, let me worthily magnify your holy name. Let my prayers be an unending stream of praise.

JUNE 14

PSALM 1:2. But his delight is in the law of the Lord, and in his law doth he meditate day and night.

I delight, Lord God, in your incomparable perfection and grandeur. I am joyful in praising you. I eulogize your radiance in a psalm.

For your great glory, O God of the Infinite Presence, I come before you to offer benediction to your distinctive wonders.

Let my mouth worship you, my heart, my mind. Let my life itself laud your fineness and renown. Let your goodness be my inspiration.

You have visited my heart in the night season, and you know my thoughts. May I be regarded as acceptable.

JUNE 15

PSALM 22:22. I will declare thy name unto my brethren; in the midst of the congregation will I praise thee.

Let me dwell in your temple, Lord. Let me continuously know your all-encompassing love and mercy. Let me shout out my jubilance.

The godly everywhere trust and praise your goodness. O Lord, Eternal One, my acclaim is a small enough benediction. May it grow tremendously.

The angels come and your glory surrounds me, Kind Father and Friend. Hear my laudation. Let my love and exaltation pour out of my song.

Most Amiable Jesus, there is everything in you that my soul needs. My happiness is in loving and serving.

JUNE 16

PSALM 145:4. One generation shall praise thy works to another, and shall declare thy mighty acts.

I praise you along with the heavenly host. Father, Son, and Holy Spirit, I lift my voice and turn my heart to the rapture of your brilliance.

I join the mighty chorus this day, Lord, to exalt your wonders. This is a special day of jubilation in which I can sing of your greatness.

Holy, holy to the Great God Triune. My voice lifts its chorus with the faithful everywhere. Blessed Three in One, no dimension holds your glory.

You ascended on high, yet your presence is always apparent. There is no moment without you, God.

JUNE 17

PSALM 108:2. Awake, psaltery and harp; I myself will awake early.

I walk in your magnificent strength. You have taught me from youth, and I have learned a little about your wondrous Being, Jehovah.

I rejoice in knowing you, God. Your presence is the exalted glory I seek. There is reflected greatness just to dwell in your holy presence.

Blessed Redeemer, you are ever merciful, ever kind. My soul thirsts for you. Your lovingkindness is my joy and my continuing wonder.

Your love and mercy are what we depend upon, Lord. I am a rudderless ship without your guiding hand.

JUNE 18

PSALM 150:4. Praise him with the timbrel and dance; praise him with stringed instruments and organs.

I delight in directing my steps to you, Lord. You hold my hand tenderly and assist me always. I am free to praise your holy name.

You have shown me there is a heavenly home awaiting. My voice wants to thank you for this added loving strength. You are my joyful Being.

You are splendid in your might, Blessed Master. I will cry to you with a loud voice, praising you, glorifying you, acclaiming your renown.

Creator God, I honor you and offer my adulation before you. Your throne is the Holy Grail I pursue.

JUNE 19

PSALM 77:19. Thy way is in the sea, and thy path in the great waters, and thy footsteps are not known.

Mercy and truth meet in you, Glorious God. Your goodness is known to all mankind. Your perfect love abides and your will is mine.

My spiritual activity is a daily delight. I rejoice in the happy freedom I have been given to praise you. It is joyous to know you.

It is a love-inspired and joy-crowned service to laud and honor your name. Thank you. I have attained salvation and I intend to earn it.

Divine God, your lovingkindness is my prize. I will live to thank you for your mercy and greatness.

JUNE 20

PSALM 68:26. Bless ye God in the congregations; even the Lord, from the fountain of Israel.

Jehovah is your name. You come in majesty and grandeur. You rule forever in power and glory. I acclaim your splendor.

People everywhere sing with unrestrained joy at the mention of your holy name. Earth and heaven join in a mighty chorus. I celebrate your merit.

You cheer me with the hope you offer, God Unchanging. No matter how deep the darkness, you illuminate my Way. I will tread the path faithfully.

God of Patience, you taught us how to bear a cross, yet our few trials overwhelm us. I pray for greater patience.

JUNE 21

PSALM 22:8. He trusted on the Lord that he would deliver him; let him deliver him seeing he delighted in him.

You are blessed, Precious Soul of all souls. You are highly laudable and distinctive. Your name is splendid in the halls of grandeur.

Accept my laudation, God, for all of your glorious power spent upon me. You alone are holy; you are majesty itself. You are my Lord.

The praises of my fathers surround your throne. They trusted you and you delivered them. I rejoice in the knowledge of your greatness.

My Redeemed One, with my hand in yours the path is easier to tread. Let it be a faithful journey for me.

JUNE 22

PSALM 45:17. I will make thy name to be remembered in all generations; therefore shall the people praise thee for ever and ever.

Praise the Lord, all who know of His goodness. Fear and reverence Him, and He will be great in your life. He is supremely magnificent.

All who seek you, Lord, will find you. All who bless you will revere you. All who praise you will be exalted. My accolades are yours.

You are great and you do wondrous deeds. The quality of your works has not diminished but has grown brighter. You are God, King, Monarch Divine.

Invincible Father, I am jubilant in the redemption you gave me. You rewarded me with eternal happiness.

JUNE 23

PSALM 9:1. I will praise thee, O Lord, with my whole heart; I will shew forth all thy marvellous works.

The love and tribute you brought the world, Lord, is magnificent. It is amazing that you ask so little in return.

Jehovah, your name endures forever. Your fame is known to every generation. All praise and honor are yours. You are the Praiseworthy King.

I pray for more humility and to be less boastful. I have nothing to boast of, except you. I can praise you and boast to all of your wonders.

God of Heaven and Earth, what wonders you brought for me. The greatest of all, love, has never diminished.

JUNE 24

PSALM 29:4. The voice of the Lord is powerful; the voice of the Lord is full of majesty.

Death held no sting or fear for you, Blessed Savior, because your will was to serve. May I praise you joyously here and eternally there.

I believe songs are a way to your presence, Lord. I sing mine in pure joy, ecstatically, for they are intended to honor you.

This day you have given me, Creator of Things, is another chance to honor you. I will rejoice in it and live to your glory and distinction.

You provide many glorious days if I follow in your footsteps. I pray to earn the love you dispense.

*PSALM 27:4. One thing have I desired of the Lord that
will I seek after, that I may dwell in the house of the Lord
all my life, to behold the beauty of the Lord.*

Lord, I am coming. Your perfection draws me ever
nearer. I come to praise you, joyously and gratefully.
You have given me great wonders.

I lift up my hands and eyes to your presence. I have only
laudation for you, richly. I seek to join in the heavenly
chorus around you.

When you arose, Lord, the world began. I had new
understandings to live by, and a benediction of hope
in the new covenant.

*Blessed Revelator, you brought us a new plan to live by.
You took our burdens and jeweled the pathway.*

JUNE 26

*PSALM 48:1. Great is the Lord, and greatly to be
praised in the city of our God, in the mountain of his
holiness.*

Praise you, Lord; hear my plea. My praising voice will
continue to find ways to exalt you. Your greatness
merits jubilance.

Joy rises in my heart, Eternal Father. I burst forth with
richly exultant songs of acclaim because you are my
Lord, my King.

Painful and slow are the steps of many, but all hearts are
free to soar. There is no one who cannot thank you;
there is no one who cannot love you.

*Source of Uncreated Light, in you all things are possible.
I want to serve and adore you more fervently.*

JUNE 27

PSALM 16:7. I will bless the Lord, who hath given me counsel; my reins also instruct me in the night seasons.

I will sing joyously of all your wonders. You are the perfect answer to life. My pleasure comes from honoring you with glad songs, Lord.

O God enthroned in heaven, I lift my eyes to you, wanting to see you yet not daring to. My heart rejoices as my voice sings a rich ovation.

Your words of peace, God, are the eternal message of hope. You are the peace and light on our pathway. My only task is to tread it.

Precious Lamb, my pride is great but often ignorant. My resolve is to use it to love you.

JUNE 28

PSALM 22:4. Our fathers trusted in thee; they trusted and thou didst deliver them.

Everyone will tell of your miracles, and about the glory and majesty of your reign. You are my abundantly wondrous treasure and delight.

You constantly satisfy the hunger and thirst of all who seek knowledge of you. You are so evident that my jubilation is unbridled.

Thank you, Blessed Comforter. You are all things to me and for me. You are my only object of adoration, the King I praise and love.

Provider Lord, may I applaud your wonders humbly. May I hold to the Way and Truth forever.

JUNE 29

PSALM 27:6. Therefore will I offer in his tabernacle sacrifices of joy; I will sing, yea, I will sing praises unto the Lord.

In praising you I can find feelings that bless my heart with great enjoyment. It is my precious gift from you, my rich endowment.

My heart fills with pleasure at thoughts of you. My voice is gladsome, and my spirit is one with the angels who sing your praises.

You were torn and tortured to fulfill the Scriptures, Jesus. You made me whole thereby. This is a most precious gift I pray to deserve.

Patriarch of Love, may my spoken words and my unspoken ideas please. May they be a tribute to your grandeur.

JUNE 30

PSALM 31:14. But I trusted in thee, O Lord; I said, thou art my God.

The mountains echo your greatness told in songs of praise. The valleys hold the love the songs express. My worship spreads before you.

I laud you who made the sun to rule the day. It warms me, cheers me, and drives away night's terrors. It is but one of your wonders.

I acclaim you who lights up the stars and moon at evening time. In their loveliness I may forget the great purposes they serve.

Lord of All, I have been given the will to use the Word wisely. It is my heart's desire to do so.

JULY 1

PSALM 18:26. With the pure thou wilt shew thyself pure, and with the froward thou wilt shew thyself froward.

The harmony you bring is as refreshing as the dew. The peace you confer upon the world is everyone's to share. The love you offer covers all.

O Jerusalem, praise the Almighty King. Laud Him mightily, O Zion. Blessed be His holy name forever and ever. Love Him and live.

The night is filled with your majesty, power, and glory. The days burst with your wonders. You are the center of the universe, the Great King.

Lord of Life Eternal, my exaltation is you. I am repentant and you are wonderfully forgiving.

JULY 2

PSALM 34:2. My soul shall make her boast in the Lord; the humble shall hear thereof and be glad.

Christians everywhere awoke to your Word. The new covenant bringing eternal life and freedom is a spectacular promise of continuing life.

I do exalt you, God of Life. I call upon everyone to join in my songs. May the praise and honor due you well up loudly and fervently.

May everyone laud you and extol your precious name. All, really praise Him. All voices, make sweet the acknowledgment of His goodness.

Your sacrifice for me was monumentally magnificent. My life is my modest return for your great gift.

JULY 3

PSALM 31:23. O love the Lord, all ye his saints; for the Lord preserveth the faithful and plentifully rewardeth the proud doer.

I come to you with songs of gladness. I pray everyone will join in with heart and mind. I magnify your greatness, Jehovah.

You have always been loving and kind to me, overlooking my transgressions and blessing me. Would that I had appreciated it more and sooner.

I thank you always, Great Spirit of Life. Your boundless love is wondrous. I pray I can fashion a strong resolve to live in honor for you.

Infinitely wise Father, there is salvation of all who follow you. I pray for the help I need in this.

JULY 4

PSALM 92:4. For thou, Lord, hast made me glad through thy work; I will triumph in the works of thy hands.

I want to keep your perfection before me always. I cannot be as perfect, but I can lead a better life. I love you and adore you, Lord.

Let us acclaim the Lord together. Let us appreciate His blessedness. Let us sound the bells of joy, bringing glad tidings to everyone.

I lift my eyes heavenward, God, often. I know your loving presence in my life. Lord of Supreme Knowledge, touch my soul with your wisdom.

Blessed and Blameless God, saving grace comes from you alone. You freed me to choose, and I choose you.

JULY 5

PSALM 98:6. With trumpets and sound of cornet make a joyful noise before the Lord, the King.

Your works are laudable and wondrous indeed. Your graciousness to me is my life's delight. Your compassion is blessed, your forgiveness divine.

All glory to you, God; you alone are the God of Life. You saved me through Jesus Christ, your Son. All honor and adulation are yours.

Splendor, majesty, power, and authority were yours from the beginning. Your brilliance outshines the sun, and all creation bows before you.

Jewel of the Kingdom, I celebrate your holiness in my hymns and prayers. You are my Immortal God.

JULY 6

PSALM 65:1. Praise waiteth for thee, O God, in Sion; and unto thee shall the vow be performed.

You are King, Lord, and all the world rejoices. You have done marvelous things. I will be joyful, singing, rejoicing; giving jubilant thanks.

I praise you, Jehovah, my Soul Divine. All that is within me lauds your holy name. Your honor is my richness. A glad song fills my heart.

I thank you, God, for the privilege of belonging to Christ's family and being called by His wonderful name. I love you and I extol your wonders.

You brought life and love, and you delivered my soul. I pray for the worthiness to honor you rightly.

JULY 7

PSALM 119:151. Thou art near, O Lord, and all thy commandments are truth.

What power I have comes from you. All I really need is enough to resist temptation, to love you with a clean heart. You are my strength.

You are the brightest glory heaven and earth can yield. You are the heart of my exaltation and homage. You are my Adored Christ.

O God, let your grace be given to me. Let me return love in joyful psalms that venerate your greatness. Let the hills echo your splendor.

Temple of my Soul, let my life be one of thanks. You gave me the gift of life blessed with your love.

JULY 8

PSALM 145:18. The Lord is nigh unto all them that call upon him; to all them that call upon him in truth.

I rejoice in all the wonderful things you have done, and continue to do. All things are made rich in you. Accept my songs, my psalms of homage.

Lord God, I take heart at your life. It is magnificent in humility and love, caring, healing, and perfection in all things. I can only try.

You feed all who follow you. You keep your covenant promises. You are honor, truth, and graciousness. You are the praiseworthy Lord.

I can visit you in many places, for you are Omnipresent. You are my example of goodness and mercy.

JULY 9

PSALM 46:4. There is a river; the streams whereof shall make glad the city of God, the holy place of the tabernacles of the Most High.

Let the heavens above praise you with sound and fury. Let everyone honor you in a special way. Let all the earthly voices join the chorus.

Acclaim my Precious Lord, you angels of His. Bring together all who know and love Him, for a mighty shout of celebration. Let all exalt Him.

Sanctifier of the Faithful, hear my prayers and veneration. Mirth and gayety surround me when I think of you. You are much beloved in my heart.

Teacher of Life, the best gift I can return is a very real dedication to live in your honor.

JULY 10

PSALM 93:5. Thy testimonies are very sure; holiness becometh thy house, O Lord, for ever.

All the trumpets of the sanctuary unite in a glad and glorious fanfare to my Lord and King. They assemble to praise and honor you.

Jesus of Nazareth, son of Joseph, I offer my praise to your greatness. May my life bring unending thanks and tribute to your holiness.

In joyful song, loud and long, I laud your distinctive name. Hear me, Most Bountiful Lord; hear my loving and lavish praises.

Lord and King, there is peace in the world because of you. My joy in you increases daily, God.

JULY 11

PSALM 89:7. God is greatly to be feared in the assembly of the saints, and to be had in reverence of all of them that are about him.

The jubilation within my heart is a light and welcome load. I carry it for you, and it increases daily in your dazzling and radiant Spirit.

I praise you, Author and Giver of all Good. I have nothing without you, but I need nothing else with you. You are all of life to me.

You are so rich in mercy, Lord. You love me so much that you gave me real life when you raised Jesus from the grave. What joy is mine.

You came, Jesus, with the sacrificial love you intended for us. At death you still offered us forgiveness.

JULY 12

PSALM 17:7. Shew thy marvellous lovingkindness, O thou that saves by thy right hand them which put their trust in thee.

I rejoice in you with reverence. I approach you with awe. I put my trust in you, Precious Lamb, and for that I am nearer to you.

The many ways in which you are great make it difficult to really know you. I can comprehend neither you nor eternity. I can only trust, and I do.

Lord God Almighty, may you always be exalted. Peace be to you, in the same way that I enjoy the peace you brought. Your name is glorious.

You put us in charge of all you made, knowing what we would do with it. If we but had the same trust.

PSALM 29:3. The voice of the Lord is upon the waters; the God of glory thundereth; the Lord is upon many waters.

Praise Him, all. Acclaim the God of Abraham. He is highly honored everywhere. Celebrate His holiness with songs of benediction.

You taught us to do unto others. It is a simple lesson among those things about which you said, "And the greatest of these is love."

Your cross towers over history as the single event of importance to man. It brought life after life. Nothing greater can be sought or achieved.

God of gods, may my life be a tower of praise, declared daily and often. Radiance streamed from your cross.

JULY 14

PSALM 98:4. Make a joyful noise unto the Lord, all the earth; make a loud noise, and rejoice, and sing praise.

Lord God, Defender and Shield of Safety, be merciful to me, a sinner. I can offer praise to you by trying more, and I will.

I sing to you with great thanksgiving. I exalt you, God of Zion. All grandeur and honor are in you, God of Righteousness and Charity.

There are so many sights to gladden me, so many good thoughts of you. The greatest will be revealed only in heaven. I will strive to learn.

Light of Lights, your love and goodness are my life's constants. Your saving grace never leaves me.

JULY 15

PSALM 112:1. Praise ye the Lord; blessed is the man that feareth the Lord, that delighteth greatly in his commandments.

Come, Lord, in your greatness and fineness. Give me peace and contentment. Teach me, lead me, encourage me. I resolve to tread the path.

You sit in majesty, enthroned in honor. Jehovah, you are supreme above all men and nations. You are absolute; your majesty is exceedingly great.

May everyone reverence your holy name. You bring hope to all. You are the Perfect Being, the Solace of Mankind. I am not nearly as worthy.

God of Abraham, the world changed at Calvary. I pray to continue to remember it was our great gift.

JULY 16

PSALM 18:35. Thou hast also given me the shield of thy salvation; and thy right hand has holden me up, and thy gentleness has made me great.

Praise be to you, Prince of Peace. My heart dances for joy in you, and my voice finds prayerful adulation. I will magnify my Lord.

I will worship you, God, with my heart, mind, and soul. I want to join in the ranks of the nobility, the praisers who revere you.

Exalt God forever, all. He rejoices in His works and in our wonder at His accomplishments. He loves to hear our admiration and gratitude.

I can laud you with the happy creatures of the earth. I am reverently prostrate before you, Lord.

JULY 17

PSALM 138:5. Yea, they shall sing in the ways of the Lord, for great is the glory of the Lord.

Come, kingdom of the Lord, embrace me. Let me live a life of merit, peace, love, and exultant joy in you. There is great rejoicing everywhere.

I sing a song of spring because I can see so many of your wonders wherever I look. You are a glorious God. There is so much to extol you for.

All glory, acclaim, honor, and majesty are yours. Merciful Father, you are my Creator, Counsel, Comforter, Friend, and Savior. You are goodness.

Way of Redemption, I thank you for the loving way you watch over me. You give much and ask little.

JULY 18

PSALM 11:1. In the Lord put I my trust; how say ye to my soul, flee as a bird to your mountain.

Blessings, wisdom, thanksgiving, power, and might are yours forever. Lord God, in you there is joy and hope; in you there is redemption.

I will sing your eulogy to the ends of the earth. To know you, Lord, is to desire to praise you. My jubilation is great; more glories await me.

Homage I bring you, God, accolades without ceasing. I sing of your honor, greatness, goodness, and splendid deeds.

The love of all mankind cannot match yours, Lord. My prayers are offered for your glory.

JULY 19

PSALM 80:14. Return, we beseech thee, O God of hosts; look down from heaven, and behold, and visit this vine.

I will always laud your holy name. In you I find health and reflected wisdom. You are my Rock, my might and power, my safety.

I will magnify you as long as I live, and lift up my hands in prayer to your splendor. I will rejoice in you, Beloved, truly loving you.

The meek and the mighty join in praise. Your love and forgiveness brought hope to all the world. You are the constant blessing of my life.

Magnificent Patriarch, your unselfishness is beyond belief. I pray to live deserving your goodness.

JULY 20

PSALM 65:2. O thou that heareth prayer, unto thee all flesh shall come.

O Jehovah, Lord and Light, I have wept before you. I now praise mightily before you and sing of your brilliance and radiant glory.

I will sing forever of the tenderness you display. Young and old alike know your greatness and goodness. You are magnificently the Lord.

The angels sang in adoration, Christ child. They knew your destiny and the rapture you would bestow upon everyone. I had to learn.

I have the Way to come there; I need only the resolve. Bless me, Lord, with the common sense.

JULY 21

PSALM 67:4. O let the nations be glad and sing for joy; for thou shalt judge the people righteously.

There is joy in heaven among the angels. They may see you as they sing to you. Let my way know many reverent remembrances of you.

Clap your hands, all nations. Shout to God with joyful voices. He is the great King of kings, the Lord of lords. He is Jehovah.

Your praise is sung unto the ends of the earth, All-Knowing One. Great you are, Lord, and exceedingly to be exalted and revered.

God of Righteousness, you set aside the fears of the ages, bringing hope. You are my worshipping place.

JULY 22

PSALM 71:17. O God, thou hast taught me from my youth, and hitherto have I declared thy wondrous works.

O God in Zion, I stand in awe of your Being. I rejoice in you yet fear to face your glory. I exalt your splendid self in songs and psalms.

You are my strength and reflected glory. I pray to always have the use of my faculties that I may fashion praises to you.

The silent stars are witness to your power and majesty. Each has a place and path and meaning in your plan. You are so praiseworthy.

Solace of Mankind, from the beginning at Bethlehem the Word has grown mightily. Praise followed discovery.

JULY 23

PSALM 145:19. He will fulfill the desire of them that fear him; he will also hear their cry and will save them.

The wonder of your love, Comforter of all Beings, is mine. I can join the angels in a wondrously joyful refrain. You are happiness.

Your glorious name confessing, I adopt the angel's cry of gladness. Holy, holy, Lord of Hosts, I sing to my Lord of the Immaculate Heart.

I come together with Christians to adore you, and we sing to laud your brilliance. Our anthem flows to heaven, to your throne.

Perfect Being, there is room for you in my heart. I have prepared a place for you to dwell in forever.

JULY 24

PSALM 89:6. For who in the heaven can be compared unto the Lord; who among the sons of the mighty can be likened unto God.

I sing my song of gladness as mightily as I can. I bend my knee in adoration. There is no sweeter rapture than the joy of knowing you.

Lord God, your glory fills the heavens, as vast as they are. To you all glory is given. The earth joins the angels in a Hallelujah.

Acclaim your God, angels of His. Praise Him; laud Him, servants of the Word everywhere. Give voice, all, to joyous songs to honor Him.

You came to bind the broken heart and enrich the poor in spirit. It is time for me to earn your love.

JULY 25

PSALM 103:19. The Lord hath prepared his throne in the heavens, and his kingdom ruleth over all.

O Prince of Wonders, our glad Hosannas proclaim your welcome. Heaven's eternal arches ring with your beloved name. You are my Lord.

I worship you, King of kings. All glories come from you, and I gratefully sing of your power and love. I will tell of your grace and beauty.

My Shield and Defender, you are pavilioned in splendor and girded with praise. I bow before your greatness in deep humility, Lord of All.

Give me success in pleasing you. Let me serve you and proclaim your brilliance and renown.

JULY 26

PSALM 62:7. In God is my salvation and my glory; the rock of my strength and my refuge is in God.

I am delighted in you, God. You give me all of my heart's desires. You let me laud your wonders and eulogize your grandeur.

Everything I do is committed to you. I will try mightily to please. I pray my life will be a benediction to your graciousness and fineness.

I love you, Lord, my precious Strength. You are my Rock of Defense. You are the praiseworthy God of my fathers, to know and adore.

King of Glory, let my heart and mind turn to you alone. My will is to honor your Being.

JULY 27

PSALM 149:2. Let Israel rejoice in him that made him; let the children of Zion be joyful in their King.

Your shouts are joyful, sons of God, because of His greatness and majestic presence. He is the Lord of Ages Past and Present.

Your name I am always confessing. I have known you by faith alone. Grant that your love rests upon me always. Take me as your own.

God of the Prophets, make each person created nobler than the last, stronger to receive faith, wiser to glorify you. You are the Exalted Celebration.

All-Powerful God, you put everlasting gladness into my heart. I share the blessed covenant with you.

JULY 28

PSALM 19:4. Their line is gone out through all the earth, and their words to the end of the earth; in them hath he set a tabernacle for the sun.

Hallelujah, O servants of Jehovah. Laud His holy name; parade His wonders for the world to see. All people, sing His praises loudly.

I have set you as a guiding star before me, Holy Spirit. You counsel me so wisely, lead me so gently, and love me so greatly. I live for you.

I exalt you, Great Spirit of Life. I acknowledge you as the Almighty Lord. Your majesty is manifold and the angels sing of your wonders.

Great Counsellor, I will declare your name to all people. I pay homage sincerely, in love.

JULY 29

PSALM 73:28. But it is good for me to draw near to God; I have put my trust in the Lord God, that I may declare all thy works.

O Measureless Might, Ineffable Love, the angels delight to sing hymns to you. They sing your praises with true adoration, Lord.

All things in heaven and earth acclaim you, Ever Blessed Father. The heavens, sea and sky, bird and flower, wind and calmness; all venerate you.

Before your gracious sight, let me prostrate myself and defeat my sinful pride. Redeemer, strength of radiant power, I love you.

You watch and know all things. I pray to please you and to make my life worth watching.

JULY 30

PSALM 37:4. Delight thyself also in the Lord, and he shall give thee the desires of thine heart.

I know to stand in awe and sin not. I know how to commune with you in my heart. I know you are the Way. I pray for resolve.

Your love and goodness are more important to me than life. I jubilantly praise you, my Redeemer. You are the prize I treasure.

My God on High, I thirst for you. You are the fountain of infinite mercy and love. You are cause for much rejoicing and merriment, being attainable.

Friend and Savior, you have generously given me wisdom and judgment. I want to use all gifts to serve you.

JULY 31

PSALM 36:6. Thy righteousness is like the great mountains; thy judgments are a great deep; O Lord, thou preservest man and beast.

You provide so well for the birds, fish, and animals. I have no fear of not being provided for, because creatures in your image are more blessed.

O Lord God, I will praise you for your fairness. You lead me into right paths and help me constantly. You are indeed a God of Splendor.

You are a good and merciful God. You are just, loving, and forgiving. All possible acclaim of the highest order is due you, Beloved.

Wondrous One, your understanding fashioned the universe. You bless everyone and graciously attend us.

AUGUST 1

PSALM 145:21. My mouth shall speak the praise of the Lord, and let all flesh bless his holy name for ever and ever.

Let everyone rejoice. Let everyone delight in you. I live in your light and there is no greater brightness, no sweeter dwelling place.

Sing to my God, kingdoms of the earth. Sing His praises, all mankind. Giver of Harmony, the world worships and adores the King.

Bless you, Lord. Make your voice of prayer known throughout the land. I will sing triumphantly to you, Focus of All Prayer.

You made all things and bless and keep them perfectly. I love you throughout each day you fashion.

AUGUST 2

PSALM 96:3. Declare his glory among the heathen, his wonders among all people.

I will remember your works, Lord. I will remember the wonders of old and see today's continuing miracles. I will applaud your greatness.

Awake, my Glory; God is King. Let me exalt you mightily, Lord. Gladness is mine, and it bursts forth in song and story to your distinction.

To touch your garment and retire unknown is faith. To own you proudly before all and to praise you publicly is a blessing I long for.

Forgiving Master, I will bring my vows to the court of your house. Let me open the gate between us.

AUGUST 3

PSALM 146:2. While I live will I praise the Lord; I will sing praises unto my God while I have any being.

I praise you, King of Grandeur. I shout and sing of your brilliance. Son of Redemption, you are forgiveness and love.

King of Children, King of Mankind, I exalt your holy Being. Your angels and I compose new songs of jubilation and tribute.

How good are your comings and goings, your wondrous ways. Let me rejoice and be glad in this perfect day you have set before me.

King of Creation, your glory lasts undiminished forever. I pray my reverence may burn as brightly.

AUGUST 4

PSALM 89:12. The north and the south thou hast created them; Tabor and Hermon shall rejoice in thy name.

Raise the swelling strain, offer up the chorus. Christ my Lord is the Redeemer. He lives. I bend my knee and bow in veneration.

Joy reigns, love abounds. Reverberating songs of the chorus fill the air. God of the Morning Light, be the acclaim of my heart.

One Lord, one faith, one birth is mine; these are your gifts to me. Ring out holy hymns. Laud my Blessed Master, all; know His divine presence.

I pray for a pure heart to see you, a hearing heart to know you, and a loving heart to serve you.

AUGUST 5

PSALM 106:48. Blessed be the Lord God of Israel from everlasting to everlasting, and let all the people say Amen, praise ye the Lord.

I inherited eternal life in your covenant. What joy is mine. In trying to express my gratitude, I can extol your name and sing of majesty.

Lord, there is no other God but you. If you were not the answer, I would be totally without hope. With you I have hope, love, and trust.

I will speak and sing my praises, Lord Most High. I live to bring honor to you. My heart worships you and my soul thirsts for you.

Crucified One, faith is mine because I see you without a likeness to compare to.

AUGUST 6

PSALM 40:4. Blessed is the man that maketh the Lord his trust; and respecteth not the proud, nor such as turn aside to lies.

Angels, help me to adore Him. You see Him face-to-face. I love Him no less, but my magnification is to my mind's picture of Him.

Glory, glory, glory to you, Lord God. I am here to worship you with my heart and soul, mind and body. I kneel before you in reverent awe.

O my Savior, by your Spirit and your Word lift me from lowliness to see the grandeur that is your throne. My life is divine in you.

Jeweled Crown, your blessed redeeming name is mine to praise. You gave your Son for me to live.

AUGUST 7

PSALM 84:7. They go from strength to strength, every one of them in Zion appeareth before God.

Glory and honor to you, King of Heaven. To your feet I bring my tribute. My praising song is for you. Everlasting King, I am yours.

I laud your goodness, your love, your gracious favor. You are the same always: slow to anger, swift to bless. Praise without end.

The Good News, Jesus Christ, is God's powerful way to bring all who believe in it to His home. You made this shining gift for me, Lord.

Jehovah Adored, you have allowed us to listen or refuse. Thank you for my sense to know the difference.

AUGUST 8

PSALM 20:1. The Lord hear thee in thy trouble; the name of the God of Jacob defend thee.

Praise to you, King and Divine Savior. I sing glad songs to your exalted presence. My heart and voice rise to greet your holy name.

I will work always to bring others to you, Lord. You merit the highest possible accolades and honor. I want to gather a mighty chorus.

I thank you for your constant forgiveness. My sins are piled high and my guilt is boundless, yet you treat me lovingly always.

Your Spirit has made we well, Lord. All blessings and honor belong to you, and I pray to bring them.

AUGUST 9

PSALM 63:7. Because thou hast been my help, therefore in the shadow of thy wings will I rejoice.

Let hymns of praise your glory tell. Let all the world rejoice mirthfully. Lord, full of grace, hear my eulogy to your magnificence.

I thank you, Christ of Galilee. Listen while I sing my songs of joyous exaltation. I draw nearer, and the chorus swells.

Every land, make a joyful noise to my Lord. Adore Him. Give tribute and homage to Him. Learn of His mercy and love. Love Him in return.

O God of Zion, I bring my jubilant acclaim to you. You are always near to your servant.

AUGUST 10

PSALM 37:11. But the meek shall inherit the earth, and shall delight themselves in the abundance of peace.

Hymns of adulation are mine to sing. I delight in singing to my Beloved Master. Christ the King, you are worshipped joyously.

God, you are as faultless as the heavens are high. Your mind is fathomless. Your word, your Way, and your Truth are mine to live by.

I give thanks and bring solemn tribute to you, Father of Light. Prince of Heavenly Peace, I bow before you. You are my eternal joy.

Jehovah Triumphant, all persons are equal before you. If I can outperform, let it be in loving.

AUGUST 11

PSALM 145:16. Thou openest thine hand, and satisfieth the desire of every living thing.

All glory, honor, and acclaim are yours. Redeemer King, let the lips of all make sweet Hosannas to you. You are the Wondrous God I love.

Blessed Father, I can sing hymns of praise to your goodness. My anthems rise to you to honor your greatness. I am prostrate before you.

Your gifts of forgiveness and acquittal are the crowns of life. One man, my Lord and Savior Jesus Christ, brought this to the world.

I will revere and glorify you, Jesus. You are the goodness I must find in myself.

AUGUST 12

PSALM 14:7. O that the salvation of Israel were come out of Zion; when the Lord bringeth back his people Jacob shall rejoice, and Israel shall be glad.

Sing, sing each waking morning. I sing of your fineness and laud your magnificence. There is so much wonder to extol, so much glory.

The angel host rejoices. Heavenly Hallelujahs rise tumultuously. You are my Beloved God of Perfection. My psalms are for you.

The stormy wind fulfills your Word; the roaring sea and its fullness rejoices before you. My joy in you is great, Wondrous Lord.

Dispenser of Comfort, let every knee bow before you. Let me be in the forefront of the adoring throng.

AUGUST 13

PSALM 86:11. Teach me thy way, O Lord; I will walk in thy truth; unite my heart to fear thy name.

You made the earth to be a beautiful stringed instrument. Your hand moved and swept the strings, and unutterable joy filled all the world.

Your divine kingdom is like countless precious jewels, such as never have shone in the sea's depths. The splendor is beyond retelling.

Let me hear the harps and let me join in a new song to you. Let me sing the song of the redeemed, honoring and praising your holy name.

Fountain of Forgiveness, I am happy and loved. You are in my heart. I give you each waking moment.

AUGUST 14

PSALM 72:19. And blessed be his glorious name for ever, and let the whole earth be filled with his glory.

You are my Majestic God and my reason for worship. You lift my heart and with help I may glimpse the holiest place. Hear my song, O King.

Consider my meditation, Jesus, my Way of Redemption. Hear my prayers to your greatness. Your exalted name, Lord of Life, is my benediction.

You are my Maker. You bring songs in the night. You made me a little wiser than the birds and animals and gave me dominion. I pray for wisdom.

In you I have a future, Christ, bought dearly. In you I have a shining example of how to love.

AUGUST 15

PSALM 22:19. But be not far from me, O Lord; O my strength, haste thee to help me.

I voice my joy and triumph on the highest peaks to reach you. The heavens, the earth, and I join to sing songs of veneration to you.

You alone have done glorious deeds. You direct the affairs of generations of persons. You are honor and might, with supreme love for all.

Your name is excellent throughout the world. I will constantly give thanks and praise. Your wonders are known and exalted everywhere.

Son of God, the well of life is wonderfully refreshing as you decreed it would always be.

AUGUST 16

PSALM 138:2. I will worship toward thy holy temple, and praise thy name for thy lovingkindness and for thy truth; for thou hast magnified thy word above all thy name.

Christ, you brought me into the very presence of your Father, as you promised. I stand in silent awe. Then, assured, I sing His praises.

I will be glad and rejoice in you. My songs are composed only to honor your wondrous name. Most High Authority, you are God Eternal.

I exalt you, Lord God who dwells in Zion. I will show all the people your doings. You have redeemed me from the gates of death.

Prince of Wonder, you are the strength of all people. Souls that seek, find. I am fulfilled in you.

AUGUST 17

PSALM 149:1. Praise ye the Lord; sing unto the Lord a new song, and his praise in the congregation of saints.

I exult in the pleasures you have given me, Perfect Being. Bounteous Giver, your ignominious end was a glorious beginning for me.

God, prepare a loving place for me in the holy sanctuary. Let whatever is good in me grow so that I may live to please you.

There is no greater glory than you, God. Your renown is greater than the tongue of man is gifted to tell. I can try, and will, to praise.

Truth Eternal, I pray to be free from sin in order to worship properly. I walk to you on willing feet.

AUGUST 18

PSALM 113:3. From the rising of the sun, unto the going down of the same, the Lord's name is to be praised.

Joy in you, Lord, is absolute. At your revelation, other pleasures and joys are inconsequential. You are the divinity the world dreams of.

I approach you with holy joy. Your splendor is richly radiant. I delight in honoring you and in offering praise and acclaim for you.

How lovely are your tabernacles, Lord of Hosts. My soul longs for the courts of my God. My joy and comfort are in your Blessed Presence.

I am free because you sacrificed so that it could be so. I am safe in you, and I am a better person.

AUGUST 19

PSALM 97:11. Light is sown for the righteous, and gladness for the upright in heart.

You are my God. I have no other God before me. You are my rich inheritance and my inestimable delight. My joy is in venerating your majesty.

My heart is glad, so my being rejoices. I rest in hope, for I have you in my life. I laud your beauty, radiance, and splendor.

I love you, God, with all my heart, with no thought of reward. Your gifts and graces are a sweetly fulfilling bonus, for I already had your love.

God of Nature, I pray to keep steadily to your ways. No one coming to you will hunger.

AUGUST 20

PSALM 99:2. The Lord is great in Zion, and he is high above all the people.

You have made me triumphant in this golden hour. Your glorious return will be arrestingly apparent to all, and so glorious for all.

I have received a kingdom through your act of salvation. Righteousness and peace, and joy in the Holy Spirit, are mine for right living.

I live to find growth in grace. Your Word, God Almighty, becomes clearer and dearer, my faith becomes firmer, and my hope becomes brighter.

Let me humbly follow you to blissful glory. Let me renew my spirit by pious reflection.

AUGUST 21

PSALM 96:12. Let the fields be joyful and all that is therein; then shall all the trees of the wood rejoice

My thanks fly to you daily, Lord, in songs to honor your greatness. I will continue to thank you. Let me always rejoice in you.

Grant me the peace to preserve your image in me. Let me think thoughts of peace. Let me kneel humbly before you and worship you.

I rejoice in you, Lord; you have saved me. Ovations for you come often from my heart and mind. My tongue is full of mirthful exultation.

Lord of Understanding, the shepherds were fortunate to see you. The glory shone about them wondrously.

AUGUST 22

PSALM 148:6. He hath also stablished them for ever and ever; he hath made a decree which shall not pass.

Bestow your blessings on your covenant child, Lord God. Let praise and adoration to you be silently reverent, interspersed with jubilant song.

O grant all of us who meet before you to have happy hearts. Honoring and paying tribute to you are my chief delights. I am happy in you.

In your hand are all the corners of the earth; the strength of the mountains and hills are yours. I kneel before you in worship, Maker Mine.

Enthroned Deity, I trust in you always. You have honored me with your blessings, and I want not.

AUGUST 23

PSALM 145:15. The eyes of all wait on thee, and thou givest them their meat in due season.

Glory to you, Lord, my life's Redeemer. You are all of life, mystery and openness combined. You are the praiseworthy Master I adore.

Acclaim your Master, you angels. Invite me to join you. I love Him in my lesser capacity, but in zeal I have no want or lack.

May renown surround you, All-Wise and All-Loving Father. Thank you for the radiant resurrection of your Son, Jesus Christ. All honor is in you.

The Holy Spirit is at work in my heart. He cleanses me with my Lord's blood, making me over to please Him.

AUGUST 24

PSALM 106:47. Save us, O Lord our God, and gather us from among the heathen, to give thanks unto thy holy name, and to triumph in thy praise.

Any day you make is a day to rejoice and be glad in. Your divine light satisfies my doubts and exalts my perceptions.

My King and Savior, you draw near. Let me openly adore you. You have manifested your glory. Let me exalt you in joyous hymns and praises.

I laud you and your works, God of the Nations. I acknowledge you as Lord. May all the earth worship and magnify you, Jehovah.

Your grandeur will be manifest to all upon your return. Let me worship you and prepare for that day.

AUGUST 25

PSALM 147:1. Praise ye the Lord, for it is good to sing praises unto our God; for it is pleasant and praise is comely.

Lord God, Forgiving Redeemer, you are so merciful. You are joy and jubilant songs, all I can find to sing. You bless me with incomparable pleasure.

Let me come and worship you. Let me know the things I must do, and give me the grace to do them. Let me live in you faithfully.

I rejoice, give thanks, and sing to your eternal glory. You are triumphantly majestic. You see all, yet you still love mankind. Hallelujah.

God of the Prophets, thank you for the Holy Spirit. In return, I have tried opening my heart to others.

PSALM 56:4. In God I will praise his word; in God I have put my trust; I will not fear what flesh can do to me.

You are the God of miracles, power, glory, and wonder. Your majesty is seen and known everywhere. Your glorious deeds outshine the sun.

Love the Lord your God, all. Love Him with your heart, mind, and soul. His goodness is so laudable. The Good News is that He lives.

Happy am I for the pure goodness of you. Happier still am I for your everlasting mercy. Happiest of all am I to be able to praise you.

Great Spirit of Life, you gave yourself freely for me. I can thank you with a good life, and I try.

AUGUST 27

PSALM 118:19. Open to me the gates of righteousness; I will go into them and I will praise the Lord.

You do not listen to evil men, but you have open ears for those who worship you and do your will. All distinction is yours, Lord.

I cry out to you, Reverent Father. I praise your awesome self, your deeds, your blessings, your goodness. You are the Universal God.

I lift my hands to heaven in prayer. There is only joy for me in acclaiming your greatness, in lauding you worshipfully, my Redeemer.

Those who believe will see wonderful miracles. You are exalted forever in my heart, in my place of belief.

AUGUST 28

PSALM 22:27. All the ends of the world shall remember and turn to the Lord; and all the kindred of the nations shall worship before thee.

You have gathered all into a kingdom. You have made everyone priests of God. You have eternal life for all held in heaven's treasury.

You are faithful to your covenant of blood. You are giving, and generously wondrous. My psalm of acclaim is only a token of deserved love.

Let your good, acceptable, and perfect will be my goal in life. Let my measure of faith be enough, Lord, yet continue to grow.

O Measureless Light, healing is done in your name and by your power. May everyone shout your acclaim.

AUGUST 29

PSALM 21:4. He asked life of thee and thou gavest it him; even length of days for ever and ever.

Jesus, you are the Author of Life. God caused you to be resurrected to make the world's darkness bright. You are my Light and Life.

My faith in you, Jesus, is faith given by God. He provides perfect contemplation in which I can come in love and adoration.

The earth rejoices in the fullness of your glory and majesty. I exalt you for your wonders, Anointed One. You are love supreme, joy eternal.

O Radiant Lord, you are the shepherd who guides us to your holy home. I trust in you, Jesus.

AUGUST 30

PSALM 76:11. Vow, and pay unto the Lord your God; let all that be round him bring presents to him.

All of your works are a tribute to your greatness. The earth, sea, and sky join in voicing accolades. All persons everywhere can rejoice.

You were, God, before all else began. Your power and majesty hold all things together. You are the true light of the universe.

I trust in you and you never fail me. You withhold nothing from a covenant child. I want to be as giving in tribute as you are in love.

Great Splendid Heart, I worship you and my will is to be righteous. I prostrate myself before my God.

AUGUST 31

PSALM 90:12. So teach us to number our days, that we may apply our hearts unto wisdom.

Lord God Almighty, you are my most holy Savior. The saints adore you and sing your praises. My voice joins in delightedly.

Lord, I love you greatly. You allow me to know you, as I have from birth. My real beginnings of love and understanding came later, to my joy.

Listen, all, to the thunder of His mighty voice. It rolls with power across the heavens. It fills the earth with authority.

My God on High, you are the eternity I seek, and you have made yourself available. You are my love and life.

SEPTEMBER 1

PSALM 87:3. Glorious things are spoken of thee, O city of God.

Love my Lord, all. God is a magnificent life in each person. Come, all people everywhere, let us sing His praises resoundingly.

Rejoice, my Lord God is the King of kings. Adore my All-Wise God, worship and acclaim His goodness forever. His lovingkindness is here.

I pray I will not fail when tempted. I pray to remain your humble servant. My greatest tribute to you would be to please you with my life.

Epitome of Brilliance, you are the Lord of my life. What honors are mine in your reflected glory.

SEPTEMBER 2

PSALM 18:14. Yea, he sent out his armies and scattered them; and he shot out lightning and discomfited them.

You are life itself, Father. You grant your Son to have life in Himself. I have and need no other Savior or friend.

I know that living rightly could be my best gift. I pray for the resolve to do so. You are so worthy to be honored and easy to praise.

The heavens tell of your greatness, Creator God. Your wondrous works are immeasurable. My exaltation of you is sincere and heartfelt.

If you withdraw your Spirit, mankind will return to dust. I want to live in you, in a deserving life.

SEPTEMBER 3

PSALM 43:3. O send out thy light and thy truth; let them bring me unto the holy hill and thy tabernacles.

I sing to you from my heart, in jubilant psalms of celebration. You are deliverance to all, the hope of the world. You are God.

God, you exalted Jesus to be a Prince and Savior. Holy Spirit, you are given by God to all who obey Him. I pray you live in me always.

You reward all, sinner and saint. I pray my life will be easy to reward, deserving of your love, and full of praising songs and hymns.

Focus of all Prayer, there is no other God. You will be my God in your eternal home.

SEPTEMBER 4

PSALM 147:7. Sing unto the Lord with thanksgiving; sing praise upon the harp unto our God.

You visit my humble mind, God, undismayed by my limitations. You find joy when my thoughts turn to you, when I offer homage.

Make all men to receive your eternal gifts, that the chorus of praise may swell more mightily. All, let us adore our Blessed Lord.

There is no measure of your greatness. You are a just God, a Savior and Deliverer. You fill my heart with love as I know you better.

Holiest of Holies, all mankind is in awe before you. I revere you, Lord, humbly but joyfully.

SEPTEMBER 5

PSALM 19:8. The statutes of the Lord are right, rejoicing the heart; the commandment of the Lord is pure, enlightening the eyes.

Your voice is wondrous, Lord Almighty. No one can really comprehend the might and greatness of your power and splendor.

I do try to live at peace with others. I will continue to do so. It is my way to exalt the Prince of Peace, who taught me how to live.

Lord of Heaven and Earth, you are close to those with breaking hearts. My joyous anthems are made to tell you how much you are loved.

You give eternal life to all who do your will. You provide a Way, a Truth, and Justice.

SEPTEMBER 6

PSALM 78:12. Marvellous things did he in the sight of their fathers, in the land of Egypt, in the field of Zoan.

Christ the Arisen Lord, in you I am reborn. I praise your everlasting name. My delight is in magnifying you. You are the rapture of my heart.

When the Holy Spirit controls our lives, He will produce love, joy, peace, patience, kindness, goodness, faithfulness, tenderness, and self-control.

Your intentions are the same for every generation, God. Every person is given the same chance. Each can laud your greatness.

Kind Father, may I be a part of your holy family of the caring, the godly who will ascend to you.

SEPTEMBER 7

PSALM 104:1. Bless the Lord, O my soul; O Lord my God, thou art very great; thou art clothed with honour and majesty.

If serving you is not heaven, it is surely the Way to heaven. If my life can earn salvation, I will have had my share of success.

Robed in majesty and glory, God, you are inexpressibly beautiful. Still, I am encouraged to approach you. My exaltation is all the greater.

Welcome to you, God of us all; you are my Lord. With the Holy Spirit's help, I can see more clearly how wonderfully blessed I am.

King of Grandeur, loving you is the one great thing I do. May I excel in it, Lord, always.

SEPTEMBER 8

PSALM 80:18. So will we not go back from thee; quicken us, and we will call upon thy name.

My praise for you, Loving Jesus, is replete with jubilant phrases because you are joy itself. My love is boundless because you are.

There is no one as worthy of adulation as you, Giver of Harmony and Peace. I sing to extol your brilliant splendor.

You manifest your glory in so many miraculous ways, yet the miracles are a small part of the glories you reveal. Let me love your truth.

You are the source in which I can place my beliefs. Let me be the good ground for the seed of faith.

SEPTEMBER 9

PSALM 31:19. O how great is thy goodness, which thou hast laid up for them that fear thee; which thou hast wrought for them that trust in thee.

May I always obey your righteous decrees. May I have true holiness worthy to laud your glory and honor. May I know how to perfectly love you.

Contentment comes with pleasing you, Lord. Joy comes through hearing the hills echo my songs of acclaim to your distinction.

We Christians glory in what you have done for us. We welcome and treasure the priceless gain of knowing you. You came, and I conquered.

You made me victorious through my Lord. You made me a believer. The world here and hereafter is mine.

SEPTEMBER 10

PSALM 40:5. Many, O Lord my God, are thy wonderful works which thou hast done, and thy thoughts which are to us-ward.

You show your strong love in wondrous ways, Jehovah. My wish is to serve so well that you can accept me, that my praise will be worthy.

Those who obey you, love you. Because they do, Jesus, the Father loves them. You are the example of love, goodness, and greatness.

Christians, let your voices join the swelling chorus. Praise Him. Let the seas roar to accompany this fervent singing, God.

God of Grace, you are the object of my ceaseless adoration. I call you Master, the Lord God.

SEPTEMBER 11

PSALM 116:5. Gracious is the Lord and righteous; yea, our God is merciful.

Nothing can really sadden me, God, knowing you are in my life. No praise I fashion could deservedly go to anyone but you.

I pray I will not fail when temptation strengthens. Lord of Light, to whom vengeance belongs, let your glory keep my path cleared.

You are the rugged mountain I seek, God. I can find peace and joy in honoring and exalting you. I am fortunate indeed to have you.

Holy Being, no darkness can extinguish your brilliance. You do not diminish; you are my inspiration.

SEPTEMBER 12

PSALM 86:12. I will praise thee, O Lord my God, with all my heart; and I will glorify thy name for evermore.

Blessed is the voice you gave me, O Great Spirit of Life. Blessed is my opportunity to sing to your magnificence and fineness.

Eternal life in you is wondrous, Lord. You are the Spirit, giving hope and comfort to mankind. You have accomplished many great deeds.

Your amazing love for my poor life is a boon. It urges me to praise you more heartily and delight in you more strongly.

Acclaim of my Heart, I have life only through your goodness. The best life is one of serving you.

SEPTEMBER 13

PSALM 18:13. The Lord also thundered in the heavens; and the Highest gave his voice, hailstones and coals of fire.

The kingdom of God is not just about talk. It is living in your power. It is trusting you implicitly, knowing you are a dependable God.

I can climb to Calvary by living a good life. Let me rise to its heights by my trust and faith. I will praise you unto my time of death.

Because of your plan and your deeds, Lord, I have hope and joy. Jehovah, my homage is to you; my benediction is your acceptance.

Cornerstone of Christianity, I want to hold fast to my belief in you. You took me from the grave to glory.

SEPTEMBER 14

PSALM 66:1. Make a joyful noise unto God, all ye lands.

God, I thank you for revealing your secrets. I know through your grace that Christ is my hope of glory. I know salvation is mine in resolve.

I came alive when Jesus rose. He sits beside you, Loving Father, in a place of honor. I am the heir of the kingdom through Him.

I will praise you with the psaltery. I will sing with the heavenly chorus. Holy One, my purest joy is in lauding your magnificence.

Heavenly Light, I am so richly endowed that I can share. I can give of my treasures and love.

SEPTEMBER 15

PSALM 89:13. Thou hast a mighty arm; strong is thy hand, and high is thy right hand.

I will respect the covenant, Blameless Lord, and shun the dark and evil. Lauding your precious name is my greatest celebratory deed.

Lord God, your great power goes far beyond earthly borders. My heart fills with joy at your presence and fashions songs of praise.

Your name is great among the nations. Your power and glory are all apparent. I exalt you and revere your holiness. You are Splendor.

Ruler of Life, you are far more beloved than my worship tells. You are the focus of my prayers.

SEPTEMBER 16

PSALM 26:7. That I may publish with the voice of thanksgiving, and tell of all thy wondrous works.

I am cheered always at the promises you gave. I am moved to applaud you and acclaim your greatness. You are my joy and hope.

Lord, you are good to me. When trouble comes, you move in swiftly to help. You are the Comfort of the Ages, Redeemer of all mankind.

Songs and eulogies I will raise always to your grandeur. My heart is filled with jubilation to know I can extol you often. You are love.

You are goodness and greatness, and all things holy and beautiful. You are the shrine I approach humbly.

SEPTEMBER 17

PSALM 22:26. The meek shall eat and be satisfied; they shall praise the Lord that seek him; your heart shall live for ever.

I am trusting you, God of gods. My life is in your hands because I want it to be. My homage and tribute are for you alone.

Let your favor shine upon me, Lord Most Magnificent. Let me deserve even the smallest part of your mercy. Let me live to bless your name.

Under your new covenant, God, I have been forgiven and made clean. More, I have the key to eternal life, and your everlasting love.

Salvation's Way, your love for me is graciousness. I am part of the sheepfold, held dearly.

SEPTEMBER 18

PSALM 104:24. O Lord, how merciful are thy works; in wisdom hast thou made them all; the earth is full of thy riches.

I pray that my life is received with pleasure, Holy Spirit. I want to please and honor you. I do extol your glories and tell of you.

You have sent me the Comforter, the Holy Spirit. He is the source of Truth, Compassion, and Love. My heart welcomes His presence.

You, Lord, give life. Some persons you cause to be rich, some poor. All are abundantly rich in you, God of Splendor. You gratify the world.

You are so laudable that my acclaim pours forth for the glory of your name. I revere you.

SEPTEMBER 19

PSALM 147:5. Great is our Lord, out of great power; his understanding is infinite.

There is deliverance from judgment because the prince of the world has already been judged for us. Hail, King, you are nobility and love.

I sing praising songs to you, my God of gods. I adore my Triune God whose words are true, who is truth and honor immeasureably great.

Stars of the heavens, gloriously bright, you are His handiwork. Lord, my declarations of your renown are far more than mere words.

Bread of Life, let me serve you. In thankfulness I will return a portion of my firstfruits.

SEPTEMBER 20

PSALM 78:4. We will shew the generation to come the praises of the Lord, and his strength, and the wonderful works that he hath done.

I will praise you among all nations, Jehovah. Help me to make this happen. I will cry out my eulogies wherever I can be heard.

Cleanse my heart through the Holy Spirit. Let me perfectly love and honor you. You are magnificence, majestic richness, and blessed love.

My sacrifices, however small, are intended to honor you. They are fashioned to eulogize your grandeur and renown, Lord Eternal.

You breathe life into all things. My reverence is for both your deeds and promises.

SEPTEMBER 21

*PSALM 104:33. I will sing unto the Lord as long as I
live; I will sing praise to my God while I have being.*

Let everyone fulfill all vows to Jehovah, my King. Let
everyone find praising songs with which to laud
Him. Let everyone kneel and honor Him.

At Judgment Day all will see the difference between the
deserving and the undeserving. Fear and love, all; be
in the right number.

Hail to you, my King. Praise Him, everyone. He comes
in the name of the Almighty as our Savior. All praise
and honor are due Him.

*O Eternal Christ, I revere your holiness. I trust in you.
You are distinct and magnified in riches.*

SEPTEMBER 22

*PSALM 48:9. We have thought of thy lovingkindness,
O God, in the midst of thy temple.*

People everywhere, listen as my God speaks. His miracles speak everywhere. Find them; know Him. His
glory and wonders can be yours.

Your glorious truths are revealed, God. I can rejoice and
proclaim your greatness. I can pay homage to your
Being daily and often.

You counsel me and give your full measure of wisdom
and insight. I know how to laud you, Master, and I
resolve to do it often.

*My world is right in all ways; you are here. My rich
celebration is in your honor and truth.*

SEPTEMBER 23

PSALM 2:12. Blessed are all they that put their trust in him.

You are my highest joy, God of gods. Eternal Truth, my hope is in you and my accolades are for you. I applaud all your works.

I have pleasant brooks, lush meadows, the sun and moon, and the stars. You gave them all, God. They and I laud your divinity.

You are the promise, Jesus, an exceedingly great and fulfilling promise. I have an overflowing and glorious passion of love for you.

Maker Mine, look continuously with favor upon my soul. I will remain steadily on my path to you.

SEPTEMBER 24

PSALM 68:4. Sing unto God, sing praises to his name; extol him that rideth upon the heavens by his name JAH, and rejoice before him.

Let everyone everywhere revere and love you. You are the beginning and the end of the earth and heavens. You are power and might.

Let religious conversation always be delightful, sincere, ever-present, and reaching many. Let my hymns be a desired recreation.

The voice of rejoicing and salvation is the tabernacle of the righteous. My jubilation is in you. May my praise be eloquent enough.

Gracious Spirit of Life, you came to bring truth. Those who love truth follow you.

SEPTEMBER 25

PSALM 90:2. Before the mountains were brought forth, or ever thou hadst formed the earth and the world, even from everlasting to everlasting thou art God.

You came before, but humbly, in glorious tribute to the world. You left great gifts. You will return, Lord, in unbelievable majesty.

I come before you, Lord, with hymns and prayers. My acclaim and devotion are aimed at your Majestic Being. Joy is truly mine in you.

All the people of the earth are nothing compared with you. There is nothing and no one like you. There is no strength or goodness like yours.

Your blood and my faith are the salvation you provided. You cloaked me with these to live in hope.

SEPTEMBER 26

PSALM 47:7. For God is the King of all the earth; sing ye praises with understanding.

My Loving Father, you have taken me to be your heir. There is no greater distinction. All miracles are brought into one in this.

O Gracious God, you continuously purify me and make my heart new. I want to be devoted to eulogizing your greatness.

Grant me your peace, Lord. I begin and end my days in veneration. Guard me from the temptations of sin, and let me worship joyously.

Those who partake of you will live. Those who accept you are saved. My faith is wholly in you.

SEPTEMBER 27

PSALM 78:1. Give ear, O my people, to my law; incline your ears to the words of my mouth.

Let everyone who seeks you find and rejoice in you. Let the seekers lift voices high in jubilant songs to your fineness and renown.

I have been blessed with many hours of sweet communion with you. My Savior, you have given me a happy and blessed future.

The peace and joy you left for the world, Jesus, is a priceless treasure not used enough. I rejoice in your goodness and bless your name.

Foundation Stone, I am extremely fortunate to know and accept you. You are my Lord of Life.

SEPTEMBER 28

PSALM 33:12. Blessed is the nation whose God is the Lord; and the people whom he hath chosen for his own inheritance.

Children of God, extol His name. Extol the name of the Lord Eternal. God the Father, Son, Holy Spirit, blessed be you, Divine Triune.

Lord of the Universe, hear and answer me always, deserving or not deserving. Let my voice make your goodness known everywhere, on the wind.

It is right to call you Lord and Master. I laud your holiness, God of Israel. I will venerate you before all the earth.

Majestic Son, let me use my allotted time to worship you and to prepare for my journey home.

SEPTEMBER 29

PSALM 126:2. Then was our mouth filled with laughter and our tongue with singing; then said they among the heathen, the Lord hath done great things for them.

Your deep things, God, are my guideposts. The grandeur of your Being is my continuing joy. You are my pearl of great price, Lord.

All glory belongs to you, Christ Jesus. My tribute is lifted to you daily and often. My thanksgiving for your greatness is my delight.

Lord God, you alone can heal and save me. My love is a shining sword to fight my way to you. You are always lovingkindness itself, Lord.

You left a number of gifts for us, Jesus, including peace of mind and heart. I can have that, with you.

SEPTEMBER 30

PSALM 86:15. But thou, O Lord, art a God full of compassion; and gracious, longsuffering, and plenteous in mercy and truth.

My mouth is filled with your exceedingly laudable magnificence. You are the core of the universe. I commend your rich radiance.

Let everyone sing jubilantly before you. Infinite and Holy One, let everyone serve you as you serve the world so joyfully.

I want so much for you to be properly revered and magnified, because of your distinctive greatness. Let the world joyfully worship and laud you.

God of Miracles, I behold your glory full of goodness and truth. I want to live a sober and godly life.

OCTOBER 1

PSALM 81:3. Blow up the trumpet in the new moon, in the time appointed, on our solemn feast day.

Let Mount Zion rejoice. The King is in residence. Let the world extol your glory, Lord. You live for me, and I in turn praise you.

Lord God of Salvation, I will sing of your righteousness. I will laud your might and power to the ends of my earthly abilities.

O Father, whose wisdom, love, and graciousness brought us to you in redemption, hear my prayer. My high tribute to you is little enough.

Messiah, you are happy to teach the right way to all. Your greatness is my joy, your Being my prize.

OCTOBER 2

PSALM 32:11. Be glad in the Lord, and rejoice, ye righteous; and shout for joy, all ye that are upright in heart.

I will set out banners to honor you, God. I will proclaim your wonders everywhere in song and story. I will love you, Jehovah, forever.

Gracious Lord, your mercy shows through all your works. You are the goodness and fullness of life. I pray to live rightly for you.

My soul can rest, for you have done much for me, bringing peace and pleasure. You show yourself pure to the pure, merciful to the merciful.

Staff of Life, your Word is very strong. It is like dew to my soul. I want to serve you continuously.

OCTOBER 3

PSALM 70:4. Let all those that seek ye rejoice and be glad in thee; and let such as love thy salvation say continually, Let God be magnified.

I bless you, Lord Most High. I bless your name and your priests. I bless all who exalt your grandeur and eulogize your Splendid Being.

Thank you, Lord God, for causing the Holy Scriptures to be written. We lack your preaching presence, but we have the total perspective.

The Scriptures bring me hope through knowledge. I have the joy of knowing and using your examples. You are my Divine Savior, my Lord.

All that you do and are, Jesus, made you indelibly the Son of God. It is my privilege to worship you.

OCTOBER 4

PSALM 2:6. Yet have I set my King upon the holy hill of Sion.

You have redeemed me by your love through the gift of salvation. All hail, praise to my Redeemer, the Precious Lord of Life.

You have said that I am with you, Lord of Hosts. As a merest sign of your wonders you fill the earth with glory that we may know greatness.

You are forgiving and loving, goodness absolute. You are the Divine Light of the Universe. You are high in esteem, much to be lauded.

Giver of Harmony, you are my light without darkness, love without equal. You are my perfect treasure.

OCTOBER 5

PSALM 77:20. Thou leddest thy people like a flock, by the hand of Moses and Aaron.

Being one with you, God, is precious indeed. O Righteous Father, the world's people outside your acknowledgment are poor souls.

I have placed my trust in you confidently. Your mercy and goodness are everywhere. My tribute of love is my radiant and rich delight.

Let everyone who trusts in you rejoice. Let the earth resound with the happy songs of believers' praise, the cadence of joyful hearts.

Fortress Rock, you sowed the seeds of your Word in my heart. Let me live to merit this grace.

OCTOBER 6

PSALM 24:1. The earth is the Lord's, and the fullness thereof; the world, and they that dwell therein.

Lord of Light, you are a great and awesome God. You alone are God, Almighty and Eternal. You are majesty, fineness, and distinction.

O God my King, I will never pray to anyone but you. I look to you in your celestial home as my daily and frequent prayer pinnacle.

I trust in you, Jesus Christ, to take away my sins by your power and in your mercy. I trust you in all things, Redeemer Lord.

You are a Spirit, Lord God. You are magnified in me before all the world. Your splendor is mine.

OCTOBER 7

PSALM 103:17. For the mercy of the Lord is from everlasting to everlasting upon them that fear him; and his righteousness to children's children.

Let me bring forth your praises mightily. Let me tell of your majesty and worth. Your full hand supplies me; you are wonderfully generous.

Joyfully, joyfully, I adore you. God of Love, you give immortal gladness. My songs of veneration are full of my heart's love.

Anyone who believes in you may do the same miracles as you, Jesus, and even greater ones in your name. I pray to become that worthy.

You love us enough to make us acceptable to you. You offer hope and love I can count on.

OCTOBER 8

PSALM 25:5. Lead me in thy truth, and teach me; for thou art the God of my salvation; on thee do I wait all the day.

You inspire my heart with love, God of Eternal Worth. You create and increase joy in me. My homage is solely for you, Jehovah.

You brought the Messiah to sit in honor beside you. There is a place reserved for me if I can merit it. I come, Lord, I come.

O God of Strength, you are my Lord of Power. My praises are thanksgiving for your gift of hope, your sacrifice, your wondrous love.

Trusted Father, you have demonstrated that you are the Lord. Your name is beloved everywhere.

OCTOBER 9

PSALM 37:23. The steps of a good man are ordered by the Lord, and he delighteth in his way.

You have been my Savior always, as slow as I was to know it. I joyfully praise and honor your blessed name.

You are Truth, Lord. Son of God, you are the mediator between God and man. May the Holy Spirit guide me that I may earn passage.

Only you, in your love, can forget sins you forgive. My prayer is that I might have less to forgive. You are my prize.

Source of Compassion, you are hope for all life to come.
I look upward to your throne.

OCTOBER 10

PSALM 98:1. O sing unto the Lord a new song, for he hath done marvellous things; his right hand, and his holy arm, hath gotten him the victory.

Where no darkness clouds your glory, where your sublime presence lives, there will I praise you. My hymns are intended to honor you.

Everything is for your glory, Lord. To you great joy forevermore. Love does no wrong when it is given by us to God, or to us by Him.

The hearts of all who seek may joyfully know you. Rejoicing will be the way of the earth when you are known and accepted fully.

Assert your glory's name, Lord God. Let me approach in humility, with love for your goodness.

OCTOBER 11

PSALM 89:14. Justice and judgment are the habitation of thy throne; mercy and truth shall go before thy face.

Your works are wondrous to see and to worship. There are far more miracles now than before, for my faith reveals them to me.

The humble will see you, God, and the godly will live in your name. My esteem is the theme of my psalm. Blessed Savior, my hymn is my tribute.

Thank you, Gracious Father, for the grace of your Son. Your gift is beyond description or even comprehension. May my life thank you.

Merciful Master, hear my triumphant voice. My heart leads me to seek your greatness.

OCTOBER 12

PSALM 9:7. But the Lord shall endure for ever; he hath prepared his throne for judgment.

Let all who seek you rejoice, Holy Spirit. Let them be glad in your care. Everyone, everywhere, heed and appreciate His counsel.

Sweet Jesus, my joy is in you, the shepherd of my soul. I pray to always merit a place in your sheepfold and a place in your heart.

I thank you continuously, Living Redeemer, for your grace and for your divine blessings. You have done so much for me.

God of Eternal Worth, I desire so much to continue living in the faith and trust you inspired.

OCTOBER 13

PSALM 2:11. Serve the Lord with fear, and rejoice with trembling.

Lord, I worship and love your holy hill because you live there. Your splendor needs this wondrous setting. I pray to one day see and share it.

I acclaim you, Great Impelling Spirit. You heard my pleas and you touched my infirmities. I extol your greatness wherever I can be heard.

Jubilation rises at thoughts of you, and songs burst forth merrily. You are the Living God, my Precious Savior, my Divinity.

I glorify the graces gained for me. May I in faith confess the truth of your grace.

OCTOBER 14

PSALM 18:30. As for God, his way is perfect; the word of the Lord is tried; he is a buckler to all those that trust in him.

Your sun shines with glory. Your Son brought ever greater glory to the world. All that He is and does made Him indelibly the Son of God.

Send your light and truth, Holy Spirit, to continue to teach and guide me. You are the Protector, the Rock of Rescue, the Refuge.

Your teachings will be with us forever, Lord, if we but heed. I pray to use them faithfully and fruitfully. They can inspire further praise.

Hope of the World, let me understand the mysteries of the universe. Teach me by inspiration.

OCTOBER 15

PSALM 72:15. Prayer also shall be made for him continually, and daily shall he be praised.

Holy, blessed, glorious Trinity, you delivered redemption. I love and fear you. I am resolved to serve you and to extol your greatness.

Your miracles before my forefathers were legend. I feel your presence and see your miracles at work. My faith allows me to enjoy them.

I give thanks to you, Lord, for you are good. Your lovingkindness is mine. You reign supreme and you are exceedingly laudatory.

My adoration asks your continued blessings for me. I have implicit faith in you.

OCTOBER 16

PSALM 97:12. Rejoice in the Lord, ye righteous, and give thanks at the remembrance of his holiness.

Let your love envelope me, Eternal Source of Beauty. You are my comfort, my stability. I offer tribute and acclaim to your glorious name.

You have kept me safe in so many situations, God. My delight and my trust in you are strong. My tribute is to resolve to live better.

Gloriously behold your people's worship, Jehovah. Author of Destiny, hear the joyful eulogizing songs offered to your blessedness.

Redeemer and Champion, all things are within your power. You are the only Supreme Being.

OCTOBER 17

PSALM 20:6. Now know I that the Lord saveth his anointed; he will hear him from his holy heaven with the saving strength of his right hand.

I will bring sacrifices and sing my accolades to you. I will sing exultant songs everywhere. Your temple is my other worshipping place.

I love you with my heart and soul, with the depths of my being. You are much to be loved and praised. You are the world's delight.

Rejoice jubilantly, all. We can go into the house of the Lord. We will open His hand to offer us His comforting love.

Spirit of Charity and Peace, how fair is your judgment.
I speak my troubles and you always provide.

OCTOBER 18

PSALM 69:30. I will praise the name of God with a song, and will magnify him with thanksgiving.

I go in your strength, God. You are righteousness and might. My rich exultation comes from sounding celebratory songs to you.

You are the Way, the Truth, the Life. No one can reach the Father except through you, Jesus. Yet I need only to ask in your name.

What happiness to be forgiven. What joy you have given my life, Lord. I applaud your deeds, your magnificence, your divinity.

Revealed Redeemer, continue to lead me in right paths.
Let the Holy Spirit strengthen me.

OCTOBER 19

PSALM 93:4. The Lord on high is mightier than the noise of many waters; yea, than the mighty waves of the sea.

Open the crystal fountains, Lord. Let the healing waters cover me. Accept my tribute to your wondrous presence and goodness.

Your death was not for Israel alone but for the children of God scattered over the earth. Accept my praise and thanksgiving.

God bless the King of Israel, the Savior Lord. Hail to the Ambassador of Salvation. Honor and acclaim Him, world. He is our Lord.

Father of the Poor, you gave us miracles, teachings, sacrifice, and redemption. I am not worthy enough.

OCTOBER 20

PSALM 13:5. But I have trusted in thy mercy; my heart shall rejoice in thy salvation.

Sovereign Lord, you alone are God. I adore you as my beginning and end. I join in the songs to your glory and the unending praise.

You live at the threshold of the morn, in the richly colored heavens in which the sun descends. You are Beauty, and beauty surrounds you.

I pray you will become more and more at home in my heart. I want you to live within me as I put my trust in you. I will keep you welcome.

I put my trust in you. I honor you publicly and often. The wonder of knowing you is my rich reward.

OCTOBER 21

PSALM 89:11. The heavens are thine, the earth also is thine; as for the world and the fulness thereof, thou hast founded them.

God of Loveliness, Lord of Heaven, you are the Blessed Three in One. Dearest Redeemer, you are rhapsodic divinity and brilliant fineness.

You are the God who does wondrous things, known among all the people. I live to serve and to declare your magnificence before all persons.

My God, you are holy beyond belief, yet I believe. You are my redemptive joy, goal of my adulation, Creator and Preserver of mankind.

O Best of Consolers, I have nothing without your love. Having it, my Lord, I am rich indeed.

OCTOBER 22

PSALM 66:2. Sing forth the honour of his name; make his praise glorious.

Your heavenly messengers help the helpless and steady all upon the path. I pray all may join to honor your eternally glorious name.

Anthems can ceaselessly pour out eulogies. None, however, can meet the measure of your praiseworthiness. You are the Lord.

King of Glory, Lord of Eternal Hosts, send me the spirit of truth from the Father. Let me follow, singing of your splendor, extolling you.

I will tell of my salvation day to day. You have done so much for me. Your greatness echoes in the land.

OCTOBER 23

PSALM 14:5. There were they in great fear, for God is in the generation of the righteous.

You bring your lovingkindness in the daytime, and in the night you are my song. Let me praise you though I cannot assess your true worth.

My exceeding joy is in you. I will laud your virtues with my song and ask all to join with harps and lyres. I will give great tribute.

New fountains of cleansing and refreshment continuously spring up at your feet. You are my morning light, day's courage, life's hope.

Your continuing love and gentle kindness are my precious gift. I celebrate your majestic presence.

OCTOBER 24

PSALM 30:12. To the end that my glory may sing praise to thee and not be silent, O Lord my God, I will give thanks to thee for ever.

There is no love like yours, Holy Spirit. No one leads so unerringly or fills my mind with good thoughts. You counsel me lovingly.

You ransomed me from sin's slavery, Jesus. I could not thank you enough. I can offer prayers and praise, and try to live a good life.

You bring the light of truth everywhere. Strengthen me to stay on the path of righteousness. Let me live eternally with you, adoring you.

God Unchanging, you rule with justice and fairness. You do not withhold your mercies from me.

OCTOBER 25

PSALM 21:3. For thou presenteth him with the blessings of goodness; thou setteth a crown of pure gold on his head.

Lord God of the Dawning Day, you have shown me goodness and plentitude. I sing of your power and magnificence, brilliance and fineness.

I will sing often to you, Lord. You have dealt with me bountifully. I must praise you, for my tongue is full of your glory.

Lord God, you are my sweet inheritance. All praise and honor are yours. You are truth, beauty, grandeur, brilliance, and distinction.

Sweet Refreshment of the Soul, you tread our sins beneath your feet. You hurl them into the abyss of no return.

OCTOBER 26

PSALM 20:8. They are brought down and fallen, but we are risen and stand upright.

God, you are glorified in Zion. You are the hope of the earth. You visited to bless us mightily, to leave us a precious legacy of hope.

Let everyone who trusts in you rejoice in exaltation. You are the fortress against which none can prevail. You are my Rock and Redeemer.

Let the righteous be glad and celebrate before you, Lord. Let all be joyous and exceedingly merry. Let all recognize your wonders.

Let me stand to praise you before all people. Let me honor you. Mold me to greater perceptions, God.

OCTOBER 27

PSALM 71:15. My mouth shall shew forth thy righteousness and thy salvation all the day, for I know not the numbers thereof.

O Good Spirit, accompany me always. I earnestly pray my life may merit your welcome. Let my joyous refrains honor you, Lord.

I will declare my love for the Word, and I will put my faith and trust in you. I have no fear, my God; only joy to know you. Your wonders are mine.

Sweet Refreshment of the Heart, refresh me that I may love you well. Let me worship you tumultuously. Let my songs exalt you.

Flavor of Life, you are the pinnacle of hope. You are immortality and honor supreme. You are God.

OCTOBER 28

PSALM 86:8. Among the gods there is none like unto thee, O Lord; neither are there any works like unto thy works.

Lord God of Divinity, release the knowledge of you that you placed in all persons. Let all join in the chorus of adulation and honor.

You are the Infinite Being, God. You are my Most Perfect Spirit, Lord. You are the One in whom I live. I believe and trust in you.

In you alone lies my salvation. My strength comes from you, Lord God. My pleasure is praising you, for I know your riches are mine.

Noble Lord, you rule the earth and heavens. My eyes look up and my thoughts revolve around you.

OCTOBER 29

PSALM 73:23. Nevertheless I am continually with thee; thou hast holden me by my right hand.

You brought me peace with your own blessed hands. You gave me such reasons for jubilation, such reasons to acclaim you in song and story.

You taught me to pray to exult your graces and goodness. Then you taught me to pray more fervently. You are magnificent and I can laud you freely.

You bore your suffering so patiently, Jesus. My only thanks can be to believe and trust, live to please you, and offer tribute often.

All-Deserving God, you turned dark and dreary ages into opportunities to exalt you. I love you.

OCTOBER 30

PSALM 8:1. O Lord, our Lord, how excellent is thy name in all the earth; who has set thy glory above the heavens.

My heart is glad and my soul rejoices. My praise to you is fervent and sincere. I am a sheep in your pasture, Blessed Shepherd.

You taught me to love truth and honor, and everyone as myself, God. You taught me to pray, and from that came my desire to praise you.

Grant, Blessed Master, that we who worship you may appear with you one day. I can sing of your glory, and I can revel in my love for you.

Gentle Shepherd, may everyone embrace, trust, and worship you. Lift my feet to the path toward you.

OCTOBER 31

PSALM 89:16. In thy name shall they rejoice all the day; and in thy righteousness shall they be exalted.

Heaven-born Prince of Peace, you are righteousness. You brought light and life. There is no brighter glory, no greater honor than you.

Your words are pure silver tried in a fiery furnace. Your words are fair and just. I worship your excellent judgment and commend your renown.

Lighten my eyes, Lord; my trust is in you. My delight is in the richness of knowing you. Gracious Lord of Life, I love you mightily.

Whom will I fear with you as my protection. I live in your enveloping love and goodness.

NOVEMBER 1

PSALM 85:13. Righteousness shall go before him, and he shall set us in the way of his steps.

I will sing. Yes, I will sing exultant songs to My Savior, Giver of all Good. You are the Light and the Way, Noble Lord.

You watch carefully over the godly while the godless willfully destroy themselves. You protect your loving children tenderly.

I serve you, Lord, with a mixture of reverence and fear. Knowing you are merciful is my saving grace; knowing your power is mine is delightful.

Good Provider, let the words of my mouth be acceptable and right. You come and my heart rejoices.

NOVEMBER 2

PSALM 18:15. Then the channels of waters were seen, and the foundations of the world were discovered at thy rebuke, O Lord.

Lord, you are wondrous and you cannot be fully praised. Power and honor are in your sanctuary. I come to your court reverently.

From day to new-dawning day, I glorify you. You are my Brilliant Lord. I have only love and praise to bring, but I know you will accept them.

I sing of your splendor's wondrous light. I offer thanks and pray I may honor you always. Hear my praise; my fervent song is for you.

Father of Song and Story, I live gratefully in your circle of love and blessing.

NOVEMBER 3

PSALM 50:2. Out of Zion, the perfection of beauty, God hath shined.

Teach me, Holy Spirit, ways to extend my praising to others. Let your reflected power shine through any good things I may do.

Father, Son, Holy Spirit; one. My praising is puny compared with your deserving greatness, but it is all fashioned to honor you.

You have made me known to the Father, Jesus Lord. I cannot reach Him otherwise. This is an important part of your salvation's message.

I put my continuing trust in you, and your help is sure and constant. My faith is strong.

NOVEMBER 4

PSALM 149:5. Let the saints be joyful in glory; let them sing aloud upon their beds.

Let me meditate pleasurably upon your deeds and your works. In your holy mysteries I am redeemed. You bless me with life eternal.

I will behold your face in righteousness. I will be satisfied to laud your wonders. Let me adore you in my heart's shrine.

You live, my Gracious Lord. I sing of you resoundingly and repeat your name reverently wherever I can. You are Truth.

God of the Hills, love smiles on you upon your throne. Wisdom resides only in you, Jehovah.

NOVEMBER 5

PSALM 103:20. Bless the Lord, ye his angels that excel in strength, that do his commandments, hearkening unto the voice of his word.

The heavens declare your distinctive glory. The firmament is your handiwork. Noting your deeds, why would I not exalt your blessed name.

You are more to be desired than gold, more precious than frankincense and myrrh. I reverently offer tributes, Precious Lord.

To the end that I can sing of your greatness, I will never be silent. I will voice your accolades and laud your holiness everywhere.

You love right things and righteous people. Let me be counted among that fold. Let me serve you well.

NOVEMBER 6

PSALM 78:13. He divided the sea and he causeth them to pass through, and he made the waters to stand as an heap.

Bless me, my Lord God, I cry. My tribute is my truth to know you, and my tongue is the deliverer of praise. You are indeed laudatory.

All the earth sings of your radiance. Your goodness and mercy gave us the magnificent gift of covenant love. There is no greater gift.

Let everyone sing joyful hymns to you. Let there be a mighty chorus to reverberate throughout heaven and earth, jubilantly, delightedly.

Deliverer Lord, let me live in your holy light. Your blessing and grace are my godly aids.

NOVEMBER 7

PSALM 85:12. Yea, the Lord shall give that which is good, and our land shall yield her increase.

The whole world knows your holy name, God. Even the heathen knows of you. Let all with knowledge have faith and trust; and with these, love.

You hear the good man, God. You serve him when he calls upon you. You are never out of his mind entirely, so you never leave his sight and reach.

By your hand the foundations of the earth were laid. You desired it and the world began. You planned it, perfectly, and it still maintains.

Exalted Prince, you remain steadfast forever. The most sacred and holy affections attach to your name.

NOVEMBER 8

PSALM 83:18. That men may know that thou, whose name alone is Jehovah, art the most high over all the earth.

Lead me and teach me, Holy Spirit. All praise and honor are rightfully yours. Author of Light, you are delightfully mine to know.

I have no hope or desire except in you. Teach me to love as you love me. Teach me new ways to extol your greatness, to compose new songs.

God of Brilliance, Within, Without, you raise and lower the curtain of night. Grant me more of each day and night to worship you more.

You will bring the godly to your holy mountain. In you I know blessed solace and joyous peace.

NOVEMBER 9

PSALM 80:17. Let thy hand be upon the man of thy right hand, upon the son of man whom thou madest strong for thyself.

"And the greatest of these is love," the Word says. The greatest love I can demonstrate is leading a life pleasing to your sight. Help me.

You are exalted, God, above all the heavens. Your glory rides like a cloud of brilliance. Your perfect love is mine to acclaim and enjoy.

You send mercy and truth to me steadily. You have clearly marked the path to your throne. I raise my Hallelujah song in tribute.

Undefiled Lord, let my life be lived in your glory. Worshipping is a precious privilege.

NOVEMBER 10

PSALM 9:14. That I may shew forth all thy praise in the gates of the daughter of Zion, I will rejoice in thy salvation.

Let me love the Word and enjoy walking in it. Let me strive to attain and live loving you in word and deed. I rejoice in my hope in you.

The stripes you bore, the lash, the nails, the crown: all borne for me. My desire to praise is fanned like a prairie fire meeting wind.

Let my small endeavors give heart and hope to other souls. Holy Lord, residing in incomprehensible light, give hope to all who live.

Magnificent Monarch, all are welcome to worship. Let your wondrously right truth prevail.

NOVEMBER 11

PSALM 36:5. Thy mercy, O Lord, is in the heavens, and thy faithfulness reaches unto the clouds.

Look down from heaven and read my heart. Let me be found honoring and revering you, praising, trusting you always.

Let your face be aglow with radiance as you look upon me, your child. Let me give you cause to feel the sacrifice was worth it.

Lord, you have helped me constantly. Your lovingkindness is forever and I can never despair in your fold. Your love is ever giving.

All living things will speak of your majesty. Oceans roar approval and the hills echo applause.

NOVEMBER 12

PSALM 33:3. Sing unto him a new song; play skillfully with a loud noise.

Lord God of Personal Hope, I bow humbly before you. I praise your esteemed Being. I acknowledge your supremacy in all things.

Protect me, Sweet Lord. Assign godliness and integrity as my bodyguards. Help me to be strong in my faith; let me be steady on my way to you.

Come back to remain in me always, Redeemer Christ. Let me serve faithfully that I may be worthy. I trust you and believe in you, Lord.

God Everlasting, you are eternally the goodness of life. You are my glorious Lord, and I pray before you.

NOVEMBER 13

PSALM 72:17. His name shall endure for ever, his name shall be continued as long as the sun, and men shall be blessed in him; all nations shall call him blessed.

Turn me constantly to you, Lord. Save me as often as I need be. Let your continuing love be the only beacon I need to the Way and the Truth.

Jehovah, God of the Heavenly Armies, help me to lead a good life through the ministrations and guidance of the Holy Spirit.

Your healing waters flow over me mercifully. I have only exultation knowing your greatness and constancy. My life is full and rich through you.

Let each generation tell its children the wonderful things you do. Let each learn your mercy and love.

NOVEMBER 14

PSALM 17:6. I have called upon thee, for thou wilt hear me, O God; incline thy ear unto me.

You are the Divine Spirit and my delight is in serving you. My heart has praise and honor for you. Hopefully the whole world will join.

Let me stand on your holy mountain as my life's exultant achievement. Let me sing celebratory hymns to echo mightily in the hills.

Let my life blend into full accord with the music of love, in the sunshine of joy. Let my life be part of the beauty of your holiness.

Immovable Rock, the world waited long, and then many refused you. When you return they will know you.

NOVEMBER 15

PSALM 30:11. Thou hast turned for me my mourning into dancing; thou hast put off my sackcloth and girded me with gladness.

Lord of the Multitudes, show me the glory path. Point the way to eternal life. Let me live in you, worshipping joyfully, forever.

My heart inclines naturally to you, God Incarnate. My thoughts are my best and most reverent homage. My phrases are written to exalt you.

I enjoy your tender care, Loving Jesus. I laud your everlasting greatness, your full measure of kindness, your mercy, your unending love.

You place yourself before me as my shield. The world is illumined by your wonders.

NOVEMBER 16

PSALM 78:53. And he led them on safely, so that they feared not; but the sea overwhelmed their enemies.

Father of Grace, I am happy in your blessed love. My hope brings continuous joy. My faith and trust are in you and the way is delightful.

My sins renew your suffering and death, but I want my life to be a blessing and not a thorn. I love you, Lord Jesus, faith of my life.

You are indeed wondrous, God. You know all. Let the unerring hand of the Holy Spirit you sent to me guide me. Let me revere you always.

Impenetrable Fortress, you alone are holy and divine. Your richness is so apparent in my life.

NOVEMBER 17

PSALM 34:8. O taste and see that the Lord is good; blessed is the man that trusteth in him.

The heart which adores you is enriched greatly. The blessed wonder of your presence is itself a joyous song, a melody of exultation.

My time and seasons are hidden in the unfolding mysteries of your thoughts and purposes. Knowing you gives me a larger and fuller life.

Blessed One, may I live to bless. Ministered to, may I minister. Gratified, may I serve with gratitude. You are the Staff of Life.

Seed of Jacob, my sins are forgiven and I am redeemed. I am exceedingly blessed. You provide well for me.

NOVEMBER 18

PSALM 20:5. We will rejoice in thy salvation, and in the name of our God we will set up our banners; the Lord fulfill all thy petitions.

You are my heart's power, constant solace, resurrection, and my unparalleled joy. I celebrate the brilliance of you, Jehovah.

I want always to be close to you, Lord and Savior Immaculate. I want to serve, praising your love and its influence on me.

My tongue will speak repeatedly of your righteousness. My heart will dwell often on the wonder of your Being. You are blessed and mighty.

My day ends with thoughts of blessings from you. The new day is a rich page from your plan of life.

NOVEMBER 19

PSALM 33:18. Behold, the eye of the Lord is upon them that fear him, upon them that hope in his mercy.

You alone, Jehovah, are the Crown of the Universe. You reign supreme. I rejoice greatly in my knowledge of you, Lord.

I trust completely in your bounty, and I have known no disappointments. I glory in your love and have become a better person.

Let my life gladden other lives, all my days. Let me serve in joy and love in your legion of followers. Endow me with your greatness.

Comforting Shepherd, I can trust you and be secure in my knowledge of you. I am much loved.

NOVEMBER 20

PSALM 57:5. Be thou exalted, O God, above the heavens; let thy glory be above all the earth.

The righteous will see you and live in your high holy home forever. You have preserved me to adore and praise you. I thank you for this, Lord.

I know that your works are holy. I sing merrily to you, making a cheerful noise in honor of Jehovah, my God. Praising, I come.

Lord God, you stand in the congregation revered and adored. Prince of Peace and Power, you are the King. You are Most High above the earth.

Venerated Lord, your goodness is almost too much to accept in faith. Your benedictory hand is my assurance.

NOVEMBER 21

PSALM 72:18. Blessed be the Lord God, the God of Israel, who only doeth wondrous things.

My King, you are clothed in glorious apparel. There is no way to improve your kingdom except to people it with persons living faithfully.

I heartily rejoice in the strength of my salvation. Come, all, let us worship and fall down before our Lord and Master. Behold, He is here.

Lord, I trust in you alone. My faith is well placed in you. My countenance is blessed to see your presence enveloping me, loving me.

Though you are immeasurably mighty, you still lift up the humble and love all. You are love.

NOVEMBER 22

PSALM 63:5. My soul shall be satisfied as with marrow and fatness; and my mouth shall praise thee with joyful lips.

No wonder you are so greatly feared but loved. No one can stand before your magnificence. Yet, Lord, all are welcome to come and worship.

Praise comes easily for the upright. I join all who laud your greatness and goodness. Let the earth kneel, let all sing jubilantly.

Your truth is wondrously right. You are truth and honor, and the world prospers because of you. I declare your radiant richness as mine.

Pinnacle of Praise, your glories never fail to excite and cheer me. You protect our destinies.

NOVEMBER 23

PSALM 21:2. Thou hast given him his heart's desire, and thou hast not withholden the request of his lips.

I have prayed to live a righteous life, Blessed Master. My delight would be to please and honor you. I am delighted in you always.

You sit on a high throne, and a multitude of angels sing. I will try to live to become one of that number forever.

Grant that I may perceive what I should do and have the perseverance to do it. In love I revere your splendid distinction.

You belong to each of us, and each can praise and love you. People everywhere can praise my Lord.

NOVEMBER 24

PSALM 22:29. All they that be fat upon earth shall eat and worship; all they that go down to the dust shall bow before him.

I praise your greatness, God. You made the heavens, you planted the water in the earth, you made the heavenly lights. You do no small deeds.

Your works are constantly lauded by everyone. I will proclaim your wondrousness wherever I go. You are the Divine Lord, the Supreme Being.

Holy temple that I inspire to merit, let my love admit me to your presence. Let reverent veneration resound wall to wall, and hill to hill.

Eternal Promise, enter the temple of your selection and design. Let me adore you there.

NOVEMBER 25

PSALM 73:24. Thou shalt guide me with thy counsel, and afterward receive me into glory.

Rejoice in Him, all of you who are His. He is perpetual love. Shout Hosannas to Him. Praise Him, worship Him, kneel reverently before Him.

Shout for joy, all who try earnestly to live up to His love. He notes and welcomes sincerity. Add more and more praise to your worship.

You grant victory to kings and rulers, saints and sinners. You grant daily triumphs to all who ask and all who believe in your help.

Dove of Peace, my love rests entirely in you. Your world, your heavens, your love are mine always.

NOVEMBER 26

PSALM 96:9. O worship the Lord in the beauty of his holiness; fear before him, all the earth.

Bend down the heavens, Lord God, and come to me. The mountains smoke beneath your touch; the world is illumined by your wonders. You are God.

You are unfailingly kind and loving, Lord. You are the refuge I seek. There is no greater hope for mankind, no greater love.

You are the King of my heart, my Savior. I trust you completely. Your glory and majesty are superb. How could I not eulogize you.

All who trust in you show reliability in all things. You made heaven and earth enduringly.

NOVEMBER 27

PSALM 20:7. Some trust in chariots, and some in horses, but we will remember the name of the Lord our God.

Jesus, you said when we called you good we were calling you God. God is my goodness and my radiant joy. My songs are for Him.

I remember the stories of miracles, but many more continue in my life. I know you are more active in caring than ever, and will continue.

Your glory is so evident. Honor and majesty issue forth from you. Hosanna in the highest. Let the hills have many praising songs to echo.

I pray for continuing worship in all the temples, God. I will join the adoring throngs.

NOVEMBER 28

PSALM 42:4. I went with them to the house of God with the voice of joy and praise, with a multitude that kept holyday.

I sing of your majesty, Master, for you have triumphed gloriously. You are my fulfillment, my joyous song. My jubilation comes from you.

You are the Lord God, and I laud your beloved name with great rejoicing. You are my father's God: glorious, mighty, loving.

You live, Lord, you live. The message of the Resurrection is doors opening to singers chanting in processions. They assemble to honor you.

Infant Christ, your victory of redemptive life is mine to use. I pray for the sense to do so.

NOVEMBER 29

PSALM 4:5. Offer the sacrifices of righteousness, and put your trust in the Lord.

All that you say is purest truth. You are Truth and Justice. You do praiseworthy things. My radiant joy comes from honoring my Lord.

You made all the delicate parts of my body and knit them together in my mother's womb. These fragile yet so durable bodies are yours.

Thank you for making me so wonderfully complex, and so self-sufficient in many ways. It is another tribute to your greatness.

Only by following you can I have wisdom and understanding. Your light is my truth and your honor.

NOVEMBER 30

PSALM 25:4. Shew me thy ways, O Lord; teach me thy paths.

I can trust in you. I believe in you wholeheartedly, and I believe that all things are possible in you. My humble song is my intended tribute.

You are so good, Beloved Lord; you are goodness itself. You love goodness and I will try to please. You said that the godly will see you. Hallelujah.

You answer my prayers so rewardingly, Lord. You encourage me so greatly. You give me the sweet desire to live rightly. I must find the resolve.

Lord of Distinction, in you I have learned the true meaning of love. Your greatness is manifest.

DECEMBER 1

PSALM 8:3. I praise thee when I consider thy heavens, the work of thy fingers; the moon and stars which thou hast ordained.

When you arose and ascended, life began. The world was new; in it I can earn eternal life. Your worthy praises are ready in my heart always.

Sweetest psalms are due you forever. Each part of nature adds to the chorus of homage. Your greatness grows in me steadily, Lord.

Let me worship you daily with songs of benedictory acclaim. Finally I may join your band of angels, singing praises in sight of your throne.

I promise to obey you. I trust you and want to merit the love you so freely give.

DECEMBER 2

PSALM 7:17. I will praise the Lord according to his righteousness, and will sing praise to the name of the Lord Most High.

You bring me out of my troubles over and over, forgiving me and cheering me. I rejoice in the spirit you impart to my life.

I show myself joyful before my Lord. Let the sea add a joyful noise. My accolades will swell in volume to envelop the whole world, God.

Let me tell all of your lovingkindness in the morning, and of your blessed truth in the night season. Let my delighted exultation please you.

Triumphant Jehovah, your right hand is glorious in power, yet your touch is tender.

DECEMBER 3

PSALM 7:1. Save me from all that persecute me, and deliver me; in thee do I put my trust.

I give thanks with all the world, God of Hosts. I pay celebratory homage to your enduring goodness and brilliance.

I worship you with all my being, Living and Loving One. Let my prayer be a fit offering to place before you. Let my voice laud your name.

Let me show forth your worthiness, Jehovah. Let me honor you in all possible ways. Let me shout my acclaim and praise your wonders.

God of Splendor, you bring dawn into my darkness, solace to my grieving, and hope to my life.

DECEMBER 4

PSALM 26:3. For thy lovingkindness is before my eyes, and I have walked in thy truth.

I want to learn to love you more. Let me continue to know the rich blessings in your love. Let me sing my sweet accolades to your renown.

Endow me with your spirit, God. Help me to find greater ways to praise your Being. You alone are victorious, you alone are to be revered.

Bless the Lord, all who serve Him. You reside in the Holy Temple, with an inviting door to all the world. I am jubilant at your offer.

To adore you is to be made richer in spirit. To know your presence is my exceedingly great joy.

DECEMBER 5

PSALM 36:10. O continue thy lovingkindness unto them that know thee; and thy righteousness to the upright in heart.

Your friendship is reserved for those who revere you. I pray to live so as to merit it. Let my songs be acceptable, let them honor you.

I want, God of Patience, to be less proud and haughty. My only real pride can come from knowing you. I want to set a good Christian example.

I publicly praise you, and I will look for new ways and places to do so. I pray opportunities will come and that I will use them well.

Lord of Renown, I know you will continuously bless me. I know you are my assurance of redemption.

DECEMBER 6

PSALM 64:10. The righteous shall be glad in the Lord, and shall trust in him; and all the upright in heart shall glory.

You are my companion, Holy Spirit; in you I grow and prosper. You lead me through the deep, teach me what I need, and let me feel your presence.

You do glorious deeds for me constantly. I see your workings in my life. Great joy is mine when I behold your amazing gifts.

I call humbly upon your name. I ask you to accept my honest gratitude and my best praises. My joy at knowing your love is very gratifying.

What wonderful songs and stories we know about you. No description or praise does justice.

DECEMBER 7

PSALM 13:6. I will sing unto the Lord, because he hath dealt bountifully with me.

Your wisdom founded the earth and it survives human destructiveness. You brought the universe into being and there is not praise enough.

My help is from you, Almighty Jehovah. You made the mountains, rivers, and streams; the valleys and plains; the sky and sea. It is so wondrous.

You are my defender and guide, Holy Spirit. In your wisdom and strength I find guidance and growth. I am privileged and loved to know your goodness.

Jehovah, of course I cannot comprehend your greatness, but my faith lets me enjoy its fullness.

DECEMBER 8

PSALM 86:9. All nations whom thou hast made shall come and worship before thee, O Lord, and shall glorify thy name.

People everywhere, laud and honor Him throughout every corridor of the earth. Praise Him for the wondrous gifts of love and peace.

Peasants, kings, priests; everyone, this is your King. This is your Master. Bow before Him, exalt his greatness, bless His magnificent Being.

Lead me in your truth, Lord Divine. You are good, upright, and ever honorable. You are praiseworthy in every way. My rich delight is in you.

Generous God, I try to give generously, but it is little compared with what I receive.

DECEMBER 9

PSALM 71:22. I will also praise thee with the psaltery, even thy truth, O God; unto thee will I sing with the harp.

You give of your powerful strength for my needs. You help me to honor you, Lord. I pray my life will use your help and guidance well.

Accept my grateful thanks for your mercies, God Supreme. Teach me to make praising eulogies which honor you. Let me live in and for you.

You are the heart of my world, Precious Lamb. Your promises are my oasis of comfort. I am blessed by having you so strongly in my life.

I want very much to obey your laws and earn your trust.
I have the keys to the blessed kingdom.

DECEMBER 10

PSALM 134:3. The Lord that made heaven and earth bless thee out of Zion.

You are arisen, free of the world. My life is renegotiated. I am blessed with a new covenant of even greater love. My joy is abundant.

My eyes never tire of seeing your promises come true. Your blessings are often sweetly subtle. My heart sings at the wonder of your deeds.

The wealth of heaven is the goodness of men without rancor, with love one for another. The earth's greatest product is praise for you, Lord.

God of Infinite Superlatives, you are a strong influence in my life. Let me profess to others.

DECEMBER 11

PSALM 30:2. O Lord my God, I cried unto thee and thou hast healed me.

Holy Trinity, to whom I owe all, you are sacred in my life. You chose me, a lowly person. I want to spend my life in joyous thankful songs.

You made my body, Lord. You also gave me the sense to appreciate you. May I humbly love and eulogize you all of my life.

Creator Spirit, Holy Dove of Peace, you are my blessed Lord. The glory and radiance you bring gives your aura of blessedness.

Gladsome tidings were carried on the wind at your birth. The hills still echo your majesty, Jesus my Lord.

DECEMBER 12

PSALM 96:11. Let the heavens rejoice and let the earth be glad; let the sea roar and the fulness thereof.

Life is short, like a dream that ends. Because of you, Lord, life has been extended into eternity. Why would I not praise you.

A thousand ages are but a moment to you, yet you bother to know all about me. If my praise brings joy, I want to make you rapturously happy.

Your goodness and unfailing kindness have been with me all my life. You are my share of greatness. My joy is in offering tributes to your renown.

Lord of Living Things, you are eternally wondrous. You are love and you are the object of my worship.

DECEMBER 13

PSALM 44:8. In God we boast all the day long, and praise thy name for ever and ever.

I know your name as the hope of the world, Mighty Potter. You are to be eulogized jubilantly. Your distinctive radiance is everywhere.

Receive me by your Word, O Christ. Abide in me and fill me with joy. Let me live in you in a way that pleases and praises you.

You are in my mind, heart, and soul always. You are my constant companion, my richness of life, my source of joy, my fervent song of praise.

You planned the earth and the heavens. In your greatness, it works perfectly and unceasingly.

DECEMBER 14

PSALM 16:1. Preserve me, O God, for in thee do I put my trust.

I trust in you and in your mercy. I rejoice in your many gifts of love. I have praise to bring you, and my heart is fashioning new songs.

High praise to you, Giver of Life and Light. I pray you find me worthy of gifts. You are the Lord I cherish and long to meet in heaven.

I offer my love and unending praise, Sweet Jesus. Let the holy hills resound with the joyously celebratory songs I offer you.

You give joy to the soul of your servant. My heart and mind are attuned to your presence in worship.

DECEMBER 15

PSALM 9:16. The Lord is known by the judgment which he executeth; the wicked is snared in the works of his own hand.

You bend to listen and find me praying often, Lord. You are letting the Holy Spirit teach me to live a better life, and I thank you for this.

How kind you are, Great Spirit of Life. You are goodness and mercy, and your perfection is mine to enjoy. I eulogize you gladly, richly, and often.

It is my joy to strive for peace, yet if I must be persecuted for my faith I am ready, Lord. You have my praise, and you are due my life.

Lord of the Universe, give me the wisdom to love you enough and to honor you in my deeds and prayers.

DECEMBER 16

PSALM 4:7. Thou hast put gladness in my heart, more than in the time that their corn and their wine increased.

Lord of All Beings, you live in my heart. You are enshrined for me and I applaud your goodness. Let me sing my exuberant praises to you.

Enter my heart and mind, Creator. May you find a clean place to reside. My song for you is my declaration of love in praising.

It is wondrous for me to behold your beauty in so many things, though I would be blinded to see your countenance. My glimpses start my songs.

Perfect Soul, my prayers are for the opportunity to serve and the good sense to do so.

DECEMBER 17

PSALM 95:3. For the Lord is a great God, and a great King above all gods.

God above all gods, you have lovingly blessed mankind. In your mercy you extended redemption beyond the Israelites. You made us whole and able to praise.

All nations will bow before you, Jehovah. Your disciples have told us this will happen.

You are so splendid, Lord, that the moon and stars pale by comparison. Everyone, praise Him; fall down before Him in worshipful joy.

Those who trust in you show reliability in all things. You made the universe and your mercy endures.

DECEMBER 18

PSALM 18:6. In my distress I called upon the Lord and cried unto my God; he heard my voice out of his temple, and my cry came before him even into his ears.

I glory in your cross, Jesus Christ, Lord and Savior. The cross is the mark of your redemption, the symbol of love. Let me laud your holiness.

Father, Son, Holy Spirit, I praise your blessedness in my life. My joy and delight are in you. Your love is demonstrated over and over.

The plains are swept with the holy fire of praising ardor. My song joins in the exultant heavenly chorus. My joy is unparalleled.

I pray for continuing worship in all the temples of God. I will be in the adoring throng.

DECEMBER 19

PSALM 71:16. I will go in the strength of the Lord God; I will make mention of thy righteousness, even of thine only.

How grateful and how exceedingly thankful I am. You are so beneficially good, Father. I sing my laudatory songs to your greatness.

Your constant care of me will make a lasting impression on all who see it. I delight in the chance to proclaim your fineness and renown.

Stars of heaven, bless the Almighty God. Showers and dew, bless His majesty. All praise and bless Him joyously. He is exceedingly great.

Jesus Christ, your victory of redemptive life is mine. I pray for the proper ways to use this gift.

DECEMBER 20

PSALM 84:9. Behold, O God our shield, and look upon the face of thine anointed.

Your wisdom comes to us through reverence. Your name is forever praised and worshipped. Growth comes from knowing and obeying you.

As one of your works, Lord, this creature worships and praises you. You are more powerful than the wind and sea, storm and fury, and raging thunder.

Blessed are you who behold the depths, and who dwell with the cherubim. You are praised and highly exalted everywhere.

Only by following you can I know the wonders that attach to your name. I pray to know you better.

DECEMBER 21

PSALM 18:2. The Lord is my rock, my fortress, and my deliverer; my God, my strength, in whom I will trust.

The glorious company of apostles praise you, Lord. The godly fellowship of the prophets magnify you. The noble army of martyrs laud you.

Blessed are you, Lord of my Fathers. You are to be revered, honored, and exalted forever. Blessed are you in your praiseworthy splendor.

It is good to live life with you, Savior Mine. It is easy to do because you dwell only a prayer away. I have only high honors for your name.

Lord of Distinctive Light, in you I have learned the true meaning of life and love. I love you.

DECEMBER 22

PSALM 86:5. For thou, Lord, art good, and ready to forgive; and plenteous in mercy unto all them that call upon thee.

The joyous strains of the angelic chorus praising you merge with voices from earth. The song provides a glorious harmony, a token of your esteem.

The shepherds were joyous and unrestrained in their pleasure at your birth. The earth was slow to match their fervor, but love is here.

The plains are filled with hymns to your greatness. The hills are alive, echoing the praises of the people to you, their Savior.

I promise to obey and trust you. I want to merit your generosity so freely extended.

DECEMBER 23

PSALM 85:11. Truth shall spring out of the earth, and righteousness shall look down from heaven.

Let me praise you, God of Heaven, with a gladsome voice. Let me adore you who make my heart rejoice. Let my jubilant heart honor you.

You reign in awesome splendor throughout heaven and earth. You have prepared a place for me and taught me how to achieve.

Though a thousand generations may pass, you never forget your promises. Your covenant, begun with Abraham, has been passed to us as our blessing.

My constant prayer, Lord, is that the earth will awaken to your blessed presence and worship you.

DECEMBER 24

PSALM 148:4. Praise him ye heavens of heavens, and ye waters that be above the heavens.

Before me lies the mighty ocean, teeming with abundant life. It is but one of your many wonders. You have enriched my life on a grand scale.

I want to worship you, and I do. I pray my worship and praise add to your pleasure in my being. It is the very least I can offer.

I pray for constant exposure to the wondrous things you do. Your name itself is praise, Lord. You are magnificently glorious and honorable.

Sacred Light, you devised a perfect salvation plan and showed me the path. You are the Lord.

DECEMBER 25

PSALM 77:18. The voice of thy thunder was in the heaven; the lightnings lightened the world; the earth trembled and shook.

Glory to you, God in the highest. Let the earth and heavens, the seas and clouds, and all of earth's inhabitants praise you delightedly.

I will venerate your holiness, Father. I will announce your truth to the nations. Your grace is my rebirth, my new opportunity.

I rejoice happily in you, Lord God. I rejoice that you are ever near, Precious Redeemer. Let mighty shouts of praise include my voice.

The gateway to heaven is narrow, but you light the way perfectly. My praise is following your teachings.

DECEMBER 26

PSALM 50:23. Whoso offereth praise glorifieth me, and to him that ordereth his conversation aright will I shew salvation.

I look to you for wisdom, and you are here. I want to please and praise you. The wisdom I gain guides my good intentions so I may serve.

You are my Most Beloved Lord. My soul delights in you. I laud your magnificence and bless your beloved presence. I joyfully worship you.

You know I am but dust, yet you hold a place for me in heaven. I need to merit entrance, and I am trying with your help. I eulogize your splendor.

God of Faith, joy bespeaks a happy heart and a welling up of gladness. I live to love you elatedly.

DECEMBER 27

PSALM 18:49. Therefore will I give thanks unto thee, O Lord, among the heathen; and sing praises unto thy name.

Let me sing joyful songs of adoration, songs of your marvelous fineness. Let me sing of the goodness and greatness of you. Let me proclaim you, Lord.

Father, my songs are written for you and sung to you alone. I can find praises for so many things you do. I want only to worship.

You will return, Lord of Justice, to measure the earth for truth and fairness. You will look and judge lives with our love one for another.

May I bring honor, joy, exaltation, reverence, and awe to my devotion. May my life please you.

DECEMBER 28

PSALM 89:15. Blessed is the people that know the joyful sound; they shall walk, O Lord, in the light of thy countenance.

Let the heavens be glad and let the earth celebrate. Let the vastness of the sea be used as an inadequate comparison with your greatness.

You fill my life with inestimable joy. You are eternally majestic and distinctively radiant. My exultant praise is to you, Lord.

All other gods are mute idols. My God made the earth, sea, and sky. My God demonstrates His presence daily in many ways.

Ever-Loving Defender, I delight in an abundance of peace following you. I know you are the Lord.

DECEMBER 29

PSALM 41:13. Blessed be the Lord God of Israel, from everlasting to everlasting.

I come before you with a joyful though humble heart. I am here to sing my own compositions, my own attempts at loving praise.

Your kingdom cannot fail, though all else in life can. My trust is in you and my acclaim is for your greatness. My hymns are for you.

You sit at God's right hand, Jesus. Your power is as limitless as your love. Hear my eulogizing songs, my prayers, my rejoicing phrases.

*I pray always that my faith in you will flower and grow.
I trust you in all things, Lord.*

Praising God

DECEMBER 30

PSALM 51:12. Restore unto me the joy of thy salvation, and uphold me with thy free spirit.

Help me to spend my days as I should. Let me live praising you and in reverent worship. Let me glorify your blessed name and Being.

You triumphed over the grave, Jesus. You made immortality available to me. Your continued glory and greatness are my prize and my praise.

You have ordered your angels to protect me. You have assigned a personal guardian from whom I can learn how to praise and honor you.

Your love, Lord, is sweetly compelling, joyously rich. Loving you is my delight.

DECEMBER 31

PSALM 5:11. But let those that put their trust in thee rejoice; let them ever shout for joy because thou defendest them; let them also that love thy name be joyful in thee.

Grant me the way and the will to grow in grace daily. Let my life turn toward your countenance. Let me fall in worship before you.

I praise you mightily, Lord. There is so much about you to love. I will exalt you in the congregation and at the seat of the elders.

Whoever stands at your holy place, Lord of Mercy, comes for forgiveness. Let my presence honor you; let me bring high worship.

Through prayer I gained your presence. Through praise I found respect offering my small measure of love.